The Advent Collection
hope, peace, joy, love

Edited and Published by hope*books © 2025 hope*books with contributions from 78 writers.

Published by hope*books
2217 Matthews Township Pkwy
Suite D302
Matthews, NC 28105
www.hopebooks.com

hope*books is a division of hope*media

Printed in the United States of America

The authors of individual contributions retain copyright to their respective works. By contributing to this collection, each author has granted hope*books a non-exclusive license to include their work in this publication and in future print or digital editions.

All rights reserved. Without limiting the rights under copyrights reserved above, no part of this publication may be scanned, uploaded, reproduced, distributed, or transmitted in any form or by any means whatsoever without express prior written permission from both the author and publisher of this book—except in the case of brief quotations embodied in critical articles and reviews.

Thank you for supporting the author's rights.

First edition.
Hardcover ISBN: 979-8-89185-407-9
Library of Congress Number: Application submitted; number pending

All Scripture quotations are from The ESV® Bible (The Holy Bible, English Standard Version®), © 2001 by Crossway, a publishing ministry of Good News Publishers. Used by permission. All rights reserved.

Table Of Contents

Foreword v

Reflections on Hope 1

Reflections on Peace 97

Reflections on Joy 197

Reflections on Love 301

Foreword
by Brian Dixon

Advent is a season of waiting – but not the kind of waiting that wastes away in worry. It's an active, hopeful waiting. The kind that leans forward with expectation, trusting that God is at work even when we cannot see it.

This book, *The Advent Collection*, captures that spirit beautifully. Across its pages, you'll encounter stories, reflections, poems, and prayers from writers who have lived through the tension between longing and fulfillment. They've written about *hope* when life felt uncertain, *peace* when the world seemed chaotic, *joy* that bloomed from sorrow, and *love* that endured through the hardest seasons.

Each section – Hope, Peace, Joy, and Love – feels like lighting another candle on the Advent wreath. Hope reminds us that God's promises never fail. Peace invites us to rest in His presence. Joy teaches us to celebrate even in waiting. And Love draws us closer to the heart of the One who came for us.

As I read these pages, I was reminded that Advent is not just a countdown to Christmas – it's a journey of becoming. We prepare not only for the birth of Christ but for His presence in our everyday lives.

So take your time with this book. Read a devotion a day, or linger on a single reflection that speaks to you. Let the words guide you to slow down, to breathe, and to make room for the Savior who still comes quietly into ordinary moments.

This collection is a gift – from seventy-eight writers whose words together form a chorus of hope for a weary world. My prayer is that as you read *The Advent Collection*, you'll feel the nearness of Christ and remember that the waiting is never wasted when it draws you closer to Him.

Brian Dixon
Founder, hope*books

To learn more about the authors, scan the QR code below.

hopebooks.com/advent-authors-2025

Reflections on Hope

Signed, Sealed, Delivered

By Morgan Leatherwood

Remember when we used to use the mail system for more than just holiday cards? Back then, days seemed to move more slowly as we exchanged handwritten letters with penpals, waiting expectantly for a reply. Life has sped up dramatically with email, texts, and instant notifications. While those tools are fast and efficient, I found myself craving the "old-fashioned way." So one evening, I sat down and wrote a long, handwritten letter to a friend.

I sealed the envelope, placed a festive winter stamp in the corner (the leftovers from my Christmas card stack), and slipped it into the mailbox the next morning with excitement. I could hardly sleep the night before, imagining the surprise my friend would feel when the letter arrived. But three days went by—nothing. A week passed—still nothing. Two weeks later, impatience got the better of me. I sent a text (which could have carried the same words as the letter) asking if they'd checked their mailbox.

Disappointed, I learned my friend had never received the letter. When I asked for the address, I was surprised to discover they had recently moved. The letter had been faithfully delivered—but to the wrong destination. I thought I had done everything right, but because I sent the letter to the wrong address, all I was left with was disappointment.

That experience reminded me of Romans 15:13: "May the God of hope fill you with all joy and peace in believing, so that by the power of the Holy Spirit you may abound in hope." Paul is clear—hope comes from only one true source: God Himself. He is the Author of hope and the only One who can sustain us with it.

When I mailed that letter, I attached the wrong address, and it ended up where it was never meant to go. The same is true when we stamp our hope onto something going the wrong way —whether it's a promotion, a relationship, financial security, or personal success. Those things may bring temporary joy, but they can't sustain us. They're good gifts from a good Father, yet they were never meant to be the source of true hope. Only God can do that. And here is the good news: God never changes His address (meaning, we can always call on Him and know He longs to hear from us), and His hope is never delayed or misdelivered. His promises always arrive right on time.

In the same way, Advent reminds us that waiting is not wasted. God's people waited generations for the

Messiah, and even now, we wait for His return. The waiting itself teaches us where to look and who to trust. When our hope is misplaced, the result is frustration and discouragement. And boy, have I been there. But when our hope is fixed solely on Christ, we can endure the waiting with peace and joy—not because it's always easy, but because we know the source is sure.

Friend, I may not know the deepest yearnings of your heart or the places where hope feels out of reach. But I do know that the God of hope sees you. He has not forgotten you. His invitation is steady and true—come to the right source: His Word. A love letter whose contents overflow with the hope of the Gospel that gives us abundant life with Him forever. Trust Him, and let Him fill you until you overflow with hope by His Spirit. Because in the end, maybe it was never about getting the "letter" we thought we needed, but about falling in love with our on-time God—the Author of the most beautiful love letter that will never miss your mailbox.

Prayer

God of hope, thank You that You are never late and never empty-handed. Forgive me for the times I've placed my hope in the wrong places and gone to the wrong source for satisfaction. Help me trust You fully in the waiting, and fill me with joy, peace, and confident expectation. May my life overflow with hope that points others back to You. Amen.

Hopeful Preparation
By Janette Brunken

Every year in December, the great Honolulu marathon is held in Hawaii. I've been blessed to participate in this great feat not only once but twice. As with any other training for an event like this, much time and effort went into preparing for this day. One way I prepared myself was to run some of the course. That way, I would become familiar with the terrain and know what to expect on race day. I think this created a sense of confidence and calmness when it came to that day when I faced this difficult challenge.

As the miles progressed, I knew it would only be so long on this straightaway before I would turn the corner. I knew when to prepare myself, change my pace before that treacherous hill. Knowing that the finish line was just over that hill made me run a little faster as I came to the top of it. Of course, there were many variables that happened beyond my control that I couldn't prepare for such as the weather (thank God this stayed beautiful even though rain was expected) or a muscle cramp, or that person who stopped suddenly in front of me at the water station, or when nature called at mile 17 causing me to run into the nearest porto potty. Every runner knows what I'm talking about. These factors that were beyond my control caused me to place my trust in God that He would still see me through to the very end of the race.

During the Christmas season, many preparations are made, from shopping to celebrations and family get-togethers. The season of Advent is a period celebrated by most churches, signifying the preparation for the celebration of when Christ first came, when God Himself showed up on earth as a tiny baby in the manger. Advent is also a time to celebrate the preparation of the second coming of Christ. We know what to do to prepare for the Christmas holiday. However, what do we do to prepare for Christ in Advent? I invite you to think of it as preparing to run that course for a marathon.

During Advent, we prepare for Christ by becoming familiar with the one we are told about in that verse, Isaiah 9:6. Isaiah prophesies about a child from David's family line. Jews came to understand these messages of hope for a future savior, a messiah. New Testament writers came to understand them as prophecies about Jesus. This verse describes who this child is. This was written years before Jesus showed up on earth, the first Christmas. I don't mean to ruin the Christmas surprise, but we come to know a Savior, our God, who came down from heaven as a baby only to sacrifice himself later for our sins.

As we prepare our hearts for him and get to know who Jesus is, we also get to know what His will is for our life or this course he has set before us. The course is rough. There are many twists and turns, and there are still some unexpected variables. However, we can trust in this Savior we come to know with confidence and calmness to handle all the variables. When we come to know Jesus as our Savior in this season of Advent, we can come to him with repentant hearts and look forward with hopeful preparation to the race marked out for us. (Hebrews 12:1)

Prayer

Father God,

Thank you for revealing Yourself to us through Your word and thank You for the greatest gift ever, the gift of Salvation. Forgive me for times when I have fallen short and not been ready to come to You. Prepare my heart, Lord, so I can be ready to trust and have hope in you. Amen.

Hope in God's Eternal Christmas Gift

By Becky Sims

Very early on Christmas morning, children awake and long to find their gifts under the tree. Weary parents—who have undoubtedly been up too late the night before—are hoping for a few more minutes of sleep before the big event!

When our boys were younger, we made them wait as long as needed for us to gather the video camera, go downstairs ahead of them, and turn on the tree lights. We would get in position to capture their surprised and smiling faces as they saw all that was assembled.

A young girl recently told me that she and her brother have to stay in their beds until 7:30 am. They use their phones to talk and try to guess what their gifts will be until that long-awaited moment finally arrives.

This excitement makes Christmas one of the most anticipated days of the year! It is also the one that is most prepared for and dreamed of.

The Lord has given us all gifts, each as different as the person receiving them. Sometimes, they are beautiful and exciting surprises. Other times, they are important lessons learned through trials and tears. Some were given through our family of birth and are unique talents. Still others are gained through studying God's Word and walking closely with Him, while listening and following His call in our lives.

But no gift is more important than the eternal life given to all of His people who believe in the life, death, and resurrection of His Son, our Savior, Jesus Christ. "Thanks be to God for his inexpressible gift!" (2 Corinthians 9:15).

Christmas is the day set aside to honor Jesus' birth–God's eternal Christmas gift! He came as an infant and grew through the years, teaching and healing on earth and leaving an example for us to follow. No matter what troubles or trials we face, we have hope in the Lord's loving help and provisions for us.

So how can we bring some of this excitement into each day as we search for the Lord's gifts? What if we were to seek them in the pages of the Bible, in the kind words of a friend, or in the smile of a stranger? What if we were just as enthusiastic about sharing our gifts with those around us to brighten an otherwise ordinary day? And how can we stay focused on the love the Christ child brought into this world as He grew up and willingly died to take away our sins to save us?

Let's cherish Christmas morning and take those pictures to have as treasured memories, but remember that each day is precious and comes with its own special gifts!

Prayer

Dear Lord, thank You for Christmas mornings and the joy of togetherness they bring. Thank You for the birth of Jesus, our Savior, and eternity with You! Please help us see the special gifts in each day and give us opportunities to share with others. In Christ's name, Amen.

Merry Curmudgeonly Christmas

By Michelle Engblom-Deglmann

Scrooge. Grumpy. Curmudgeonly. These are words that might describe the local bell maker in my small Minnesota hometown around Christmas time. He's my dad. Yet behind the gruff exterior, something quietly beautiful was always at work.

Every Christmas, for thirty-seven years, he would dedicate himself to making hundreds of tiny bells in his machine shop. For months, he sketched, tested, and reshaped a new design −grinding and polishing intricate creations that became more beautiful every year. It often became a task, an obligation, a Christmas expectation. You know the kind. Deadlines loomed, expectations weighed heavily. People anticipated the bells. Collected them. Demanded them. But as each bell came to life, as his hands shaped the metal into something delicate and ringing, the work transformed. What began each year as duty became more−something meaningful, threaded with love, care, and the quiet spirit of Christmas.

Each year, family and friends from the community would gather with him in assembly lines to twist, hammer, thread, and tie the bells together. The little "elves" would come to assemble bells, crafting joy together. These bells, many sold at the local church, became treasured gifts and, quite simply, tradition. But the true magic wasn't in the objects themselves—it was in the life they carried.

Hidden in the smallest moments, the bells brought Christmas spirit: slipped into the hands of a waitress, left on a counter for a teller, discovered by a neighbor, slipped into a bag of a fellow Scrooge doing last-minute Christmas shopping. The bells carried joy, surprise, connection, and hope. Hope that in these sweet little rings, he and others would find the Christmas spirit that often gets buried under obligation and expectation. Over the years, my dad would share these encounters with me—of eyes lighting up, shoulders relaxing, hearts quietly lifting. It's where we found God in the busy season of Christmas. The true meaning of Christmas. As distance separated us, the phone would connect us, sharing stories of finding God in the Christmas season, in the most delicate and unsuspecting places.

This season, watch for the little things.

The laugh that cuts through a hard day.

The kindness that catches you off guard.

The resilience that blooms where no one expects it.

The little bell that finds its way into your palm,

and from your palm, into your heart.

This is hope.

Not loud. Not polished. Ordinary. Human.

A warmth that seeps through the curmudgeonly heaviness of Christmas expectation.

Even my dad—the one they called Scrooge, the man who grumbled as he worked for months in his shop—knew this truth. What began as duty became devotion. Grumbling became grace. Expectation became a gift of Christmas spirit. Each bell he made carried a spark of hope: hope that joy could reach the weary, love could touch the overlooked, the ordinary could be extraordinary. A tiny reminder that Christmas spirit, hope, and love often arrive softly, in the cracks, in the grumpies, in the smallest gifts we give—and receive. There, we find Christmas.

In every soft ring of those little bells was an invitation to pause, to listen, to remember that God is near. Advent hope often arrives this way—quietly, gently, unexpectedly—reminding us of the psalmist's words: "Be still, and know that I am God" (Psalm 46:10). In the stillness, we find Him. Friends, Christmas is coming.

*My dad, Dan Engblom, is also an author in this Hope section, as is my daughter, Claire Deglmann; three generations of hope.

Prayer

God of Advent, let me hear hope's gentle call in the world around me—in bells, in laughter, in unexpected kindness. May it remind me that light, love, and Christmas spirit are always near, waiting to be noticed, held, and shared. Amen.

Hope in my Pocket:
A Christmas List

By Daniel J. Engblom

As a child, the weeks before Christmas were filled with anticipation. Advent was a time of Christmas lists gleaned from the pages of a Sears and Roebuck catalog. Popcorn garland was strung and hung on a "good enough" spruce, precariously perched in the corner of the living room. Mysteriously, gifts appeared under the tree. The anticipation mounted with each beribboned box.

All too soon, these fanciful trappings of the season were pushed aside by schedules and responsibilities, borne by the yoke of adulting. Advent took on a chaotic nature, and I lost sight of the reason for the season.

My joyful anticipation succumbed to a curmudgeonly disposition. I felt like Scrooge, and I was miserable, but not hopelessly miserable. After all, the hope of the Advent season is in God's faithfulness and in the certainty that God fulfills what God promises.

We drag around our brokenness in the same container as our holiness.

So, I went back to what worked as a kid. A Christmas list. Not a wish list of items that could be brightly packaged and tucked under a tree, but a conscious, watchful list, recording the encounters that brought me joy. I took note of these on a slip of paper that I carried in my pocket everywhere I went during Advent and on through the 12 days of Christmas. Included on these lists have been things like: the random kindness of a stranger, children singing, a chance meeting with an old friend, and a simple smile in passing. For me, this "Christmas list" becomes a tangible way to practice the watchfulness that is at the very heart of the Advent season.

Watchfulness during Advent is a preparation of the heart for Christmas. As a result, my curmudgeonly disposition softened, my "Bah! Humbugs!" were replaced by "Ah! There's God!"

The following words, from something I wrote nearly 60 years ago, come to mind. They seem mysteriously appropriate in this context. (I've learned to listen to the mysterious guidance of the Holy Spirit, so I offer them up here.) "Quiet as the stillness of the night is love as it heals the unseeable wounds and forgets the unforgettable memories. The fog lifts. The memories fade. Soon the eyes of the present no longer see the world through a blanket of fog but behold with clearness the complexities of life and oh, the peacefulness of love."

From 1 John 4:16: "So we have come to know and to believe the love that God has for us. God is love, and whoever abides in love abides in God, and God abides in him."

If then, God IS love:

"But we have this treasure in jars of clay, to show that the surpassing power belongs to God and not to us." (2 Corinthians 4:7).

Prayer

May the transformative power of God that dwells within us as the all-surpassing power of the Holy Spirit, fill our pockets, our lists, our clay jars with blessings that give us pause to smile, to reflect, and give thanks. In so doing, may we rise above the brokenness and embrace the treasure that is Jesus Christ, who abides in us. Amen

More than a Name
By Claire Deglmann

The couple sat in the lobby of the doctor's office waiting for the news. Their fingers laced together. Glances of nervousness, hand squeezes of excitement, legs bouncing with anticipation. A nurse invited them into the small exam room. They held hands anxiously, waiting for the results.

They cried.

They prayed.

They hoped.

The couple held one another as the doctor came out. They wanted a child for so long.

After years of trying to have a baby, they were tired. Desperate. Overwhelmed. Losing hope. Her hand shook as the doctor handed her the pregnancy test. It said "pregnant." She turned to her husband in disbelief. It seemed hard to believe. It seemed impossible. "Pregnant?" she said, "Are you sure?" The doctor smiled reassuringly and nodded. The husband seemed stunned. Could this be true? Finally true? They had wanted a child for years, and after a miscarriage, this seemed unreal. He wanted to believe it. The wife put her head in her hands and cried tears of joy and relief. They embraced each other, sharing a moment of connection.

The losses they had experienced on their way to becoming pregnant made them scared of what could happen. Over the next few months, they had people praying for them, and when they experienced fear, the others would hold hope for the growing baby. Friends and family in their church prayed for them, helping them to remain hopeful.

As the baby grew inside her...
They prepared their minds
Hearts
For a life of busy and new

Holding space for
Excitement
Fear
Expectations
Hope

They held each other in silence
They persevered through fear
They weren't alone
They had God
They cried
They prayed
They hoped

The baby was growing and healthy. The path was clear and bright. Finally, the day arrived. They traveled to the hospital, prepared and hopeful. They welcomed a baby, one that had been prayed for by many, into this world.

A precious baby girl.
The girl they had wanted for so long.
The tiny baby that they held so much love for.
That so many had prayed for.
This was the girl that had brought so much
Hope
Love
Compassion
Community
Togetherness.

When they saw her, pieces assembled and shifted, the world held its breath. All of the hope, whispered prayers and tears they shed had been answered. They knew what to name her. Claire Hope.

This happened thirteen years ago. I am Claire Hope. This is my story.

Prayer

Lord, help us to notice miracles big and small today. Even though in this story the miracle is big, they aren't always. Help us keep hope in You and know that You are always with us. Even if it feels like we are alone, help us know that we are never alone because You are always with us. Amen.

Living in the "In Between"

By Stephanie Gavel

There is an enormous amount of heaviness in the world today. There are greater efforts and more money spent on the pursuit of happiness, and yet, fewer happy people. There are wars, staggering accounts of sex trafficking, assassinations, people persecuted for their faith, mass shootings, devalued human life, depression, families breaking apart, and the list goes on and on. It is easy to reflect on the state of the world and think that there is no hope.

Except for Jesus. God's response to our brokenness always has been and always will be Jesus. Emmanuel, God with us. He came quietly under the cover of night, born in a humble and dirty stable, innocent of all charges that would one day be placed on his shoulders. Every year, we celebrate His birth, but do we run as fast as we can through the season, gasping for nourishment, or do we pause and drink in the hope available to us in Christ?

Quite a number of years ago, I was going through all the preparations for Christmas when I confided in a dear friend of mine that I was really struggling. I was in a dark place and felt empty. What I saw in the future was just more of the same...and it was not good. The situation that I was in felt completely hopeless and I longed to see something that would give me hope. I did not get the answer to my prayers that I wanted or expected, but I did get what I needed. The reminder through a sweet Word of God that where my hope rests is what will determine whether I live out of abundance or out of emptiness.

The beautiful prayer uttered by Paul, in Romans 15:13, reminded me that I have a role in my relationship with God, and that is one of trust. God is so generous. He does not want us to live as one scraping by on crumbs, but instead live nourished, drenched, overflowing with hope. The truth is that we often do not receive what God so generously wants to give us because we withhold our trust.

The hope that Paul is referencing is not a whimsical wish as the world thinks of hope. If we truly believe and trust that Jesus is our One and Only Lord and Savior, then we have a hope that cannot be destroyed or dismissed. This hope equips us to live with assurance, confidence, and expectation. Nothing can satisfy what our soul craves except for Jesus Christ, the Messiah, Emmanuel. Our Savior and Redeemer. God with us.

The messes of life can be overwhelming, but when Jesus owns your heart, hope flows and it flows in abundance. Even if the prayers that you have uttered go unanswered, when Jesus owns your heart, hope flows, and it flows in abundance. This Advent season, won't you receive what God wants to give you so generously by fully trusting in Him? May we not live from emptiness; instead, let us choose to live in abundance because Jesus has come and is coming again! He is our hope and the One we hope in!

Prayer

Lord God, I pray that we would overflow with the abundance of hope through the power of your Holy Spirit and that we may live in true joy and peace this Christmas season in a way that we never have before. As we wait on Your Son's return, help us to live in complete reliance on and trust in You. In Your Son's sweet name, Our Savior and Redeemer, Jesus Christ. Amen.

Night Lights and the Holy Light

By Brianna Barrett

*E*arlier this year, I experienced some neurological health issues that caused dizziness and balance problems, mimicking a stroke. As I was recovering, my rehab provider explained I needed to have light everywhere because when I closed my eyes—creating darkness—I stumbled and fell. At night, I needed to add night lights and make sure to always illuminate my walking path. Her advice rang true, not just for my neurological issues, but in my entire life. When we lose our light, it dims, or when we fall into the darkness, it's easy to stumble and fall.

Jesus came during a dark time many years ago, during a time of political unrest, and He illuminated a new path, becoming the light of the world.

Winter is a dark season because of the longer nights, the added stress of the holidays, and the loneliness that the holidays can cause. But at Christmas, lights and candles light up the streets and homes, creating dancing lights against the darkness. Christmas lights can light an entire room, bringing it from complete darkness to light. Jesus is like that. He came into the world to bring light/goodness into the world, expelling the darkness. Light always conquers darkness.

Christmas is a beautiful time of year with the added cheer of the lights adorning houses, yards, and trees, but Jesus is the light we need to combat all the darkness in this world. Jesus told the people, "'I am the light of the world. Whoever follows me will not walk in darkness, but will have the light of life'" (John 8:12b). Jesus spoke these words during the Feast of Shelters, which is a Jewish festival commemorating the Israelite's shelters during their exodus from Egypt. Today, Jews still celebrate this festival as a time to celebrate God's provision.

Jesus calls Himself the light of the world because He is the light revealing God. King David shares in Psalm 27:1, "The Lord is my light and my salvation; whom shall I fear? The Lord is the stronghold of my life; of whom shall I be afraid?" We needed the light of the world in order to be saved, and the Lord provided it. He protects those who believe.

Some lights warn us of dangers. Brake lights, the check engine light, and emergency vehicle lights remind us to slow down, check something, or even redirect our path to avoid some hazard. Jesus can be a warning light to keep us away from sin.

My mind was chaotic as I stumbled through the night, but my night light combated the darkness, provided safety and security, and helped me keep my balance. Jesus brings order to the chaos and He is our light. Knowing that in my spiritual life, when I'm not trusting and being obedient to the Lord, it's easy to fall and stumble into the darkness (sin). I want to remember that my light shines so others can see too. I want to trust the Lord with this season and shine brightly for those that I encounter.

This holiday season, is your trust in the Lord? Are you allowing Him to light your path, following Him boldly and obediently? Make sure Jesus is lighting your path so you don't stumble and fall, and make sure your light shines bright to help illuminate the path for others.

Prayer

Lord, thank You for being the light in this dark world, illuminating my way. Help me shine brightly for others to see You through me. Thank You for Your word being a lamp to light my path. In Jesus' name. Amen.

Hope in the Ordinary

By Sherri S. Autrey

Everything was ordinary about that night. The sheep had grazed all day, and now the shepherds were gathering them into the sheepfold. As they went about their normal routines, maybe the shepherds were chatting with one another about their day or possibly about their families. Or maybe they were silent. But most assuredly, they were focusing on the mundane rhythms that defined their days.

Little did they know that their ordinary lives were seen by an extraordinary God whose glory was about to split open the night sky and change their hearts forever!

The shepherds weren't doing anything unusual as they went about their tasks in their dusty sandals and grass-stained clothes. They weren't stepping outside of their commonplace circumstances or thinking about working hard to earn favor with God.

Instead, the shepherds were just being faithful in doing the normal things required of them each day. And amid the ordinary, God bridged the distance between the heavenly realms and the Bethlehem hillside. He filled the night with the sounds of angels declaring that Hope had arrived in a baby boy named Jesus!

Like the shepherds, we also have daily routines that require our attention and demand our time. We often struggle to find the energy to check one more thing off our long list of responsibilities. We're accustomed to thinking that if we try hard enough, everything will finally fall into place. Self-efforts and overthinking litter our days with false expectations and exhausted minds.

We "hope" we can get the house cleaned by Friday. We "hope" it doesn't rain during our weekend beach trip. We "hope" we can meet our work deadline.

But God's hope is not based on wishful thinking nor hindered by messy circumstances. It's not dependent upon our productivity, resilience, or abilities. Instead, His hope is a gift wrapped in grace and lavished with love.

The hope that Jesus brought to the shepherds on that long-ago night is the same Hope that shatters our every fear and turns the ordinary into the miraculous. This is the hope of confident expectation. Because no matter what, we can always trust that He sees us right where we are.

He is the Hope that never stops showing up in the mundane, the minuscule, and the messy. He is the Hope that transcends all our efforts and all our mistakes. When Jesus enters our dark night, nothing is ever the same again! He is the same Hope that arrived in a noisy, dusty stable and caused shepherds to praise and angels to sing. And He will always keep coming. Keep loving. Keep raining down grace.

Jesus holds the key to the only Hope that matters. Even when our days seem dull or we feel unseen, He keeps entering our world in unexpected ways. He is our most amazing gift! May we never stop praising Him for His extraordinary Hope, sent from heaven above into the middle of our ordinary lives!

Prayer

God, thank you for seeing us in the middle of our ordinary lives and offering us your precious gift of Hope. We praise you for meeting us in our mess and shining your light into our darkest night. Forgive us when our faith is too small and help us to never lose sight of your holy offering of hope. Amen.

Hope Has a Name

By Lauren Cantrell

True hope never disappoints. It mends the deepest wounds and stands the test of time. But hope is not a concept or a feeling—it is a person. Two thousand years ago, Hope walked dusty roads, spoke to outcasts, healed the broken, and carried a cross meant for us. He taught us that earth-shattering love gives birth to unshakable hope that calls us to something greater: truth, perseverance, and courage. It whispers that every step we take has purpose, even when the path feels uncertain. Yet we must ask: Who is behind our hope? Is it Christ, or something counterfeit? The difference is everything.

To be rooted in Christ is to be unmovable, like a tree whose roots sink deep into living water. But false hope, no matter how comforting it may seem, cannot withstand the storm. I have learned this not from theory, but through life itself, through the ordinary rhythms of school, the refining lessons of marriage, and the anticipation of a child yet to come.

There were seasons when gratitude felt impossible, when I couldn't see the next step, when prayers seemed to fall silent. Yet those were the very places where true hope was born. Paul reminds us in Romans 5:3-5 that the Spirit enables us to live according to God's promises, even in suffering, showing that hope is not fleeting but steadfast.

Hope, I've learned, grows in the soil of suffering. It blooms from the ashes of what we cannot control. It is built, not in comfort, but in the crucible of surrender. Hope comes quietly, sometimes in a thousand little thank-yous. The breath in our lungs, the sunrise after a sleepless night, the arms that still hold us when we falter. It comes when we finally understand that we deserve nothing, yet have been given everything.

We are but dust, and still, God calls us beloved. Our righteousness is filthy rags, yet His mercy clothes us in grace. Each moment we live in that awareness, hope deepens. Slowly, steadily, it roots itself within us until even in heartbreak, we know we are not forsaken.

True hope heals because it is anchored in the One who conquered death. It reminds us that every ache is temporary, every loss redeemed, every tear noted. To live in this kind of hope is not to escape pain but to see through it, to recognize Christ's presence in the waiting, His strength in weakness, His purpose in the unknown.

So today, when the world feels fragile, remember: Hope still walks among us. He still speaks. He still heals. He is enough.

Prayer

Lord Jesus, we invite You to transform our hearts today. Give us grace to listen, understand, and see how undeserving we are of Your agape love. Help us remember that You not merely the source of our hope, You ARE Hope. Teach us to seek Your face and grow through every season, even the ones that bring us to our knees. Let hope take root and bloom into lasting joy, amen.

Longing for Home: An Advent Journey

By Stacey Glass

Going through difficult times can take your breath away, especially when several challenges come all at once. In July 2023, my family faced one of those moments that forever changed our lives. I had just put on my pajamas and was lying in bed. My husband, Eric, was still in the bathroom getting ready to join me. Suddenly, the shrill sound of the smoke alarms rang through the house. As Eric stepped out of our bedroom, the alarms briefly stopped, only to blare again moments later, sending a chilling urgency through the air.

Eric rushed to the garage and opened the door—his heart sank when he saw an electric scooter engulfed in flames. Without hesitation, he grabbed the fire extinguisher and tried to put out the fire, but was quickly overtaken by smoke. Meanwhile, our son was calling 911. We evacuated immediately, stepping outside with nothing but the clothes we wore. Our home is far from the nearest fire station, so the wait for firefighters felt agonizingly long—over ten minutes—as thick smoke poured from the garage.

By the time the fire crew arrived, the garage door was warping from the heat. They quickly cut the door in half, extinguished the fire, and submerged the scooter's battery in water, preventing a potential disaster. Though the fire was confined to the garage, smoke had infiltrated nearly every corner of our home, and the damage was worse than we had imagined.

We were initially told we'd be displaced for about six weeks, but the repairs required us to move out entirely. After nearly a month waiting for the restoration company to pack our belongings, the reality set in—it wouldn't be a quick fix.

As Christmas approached, our hearts hoped we'd be back home to celebrate. Christmas is my favorite time of the year. I love having family gather, hearing the laughter as we decorate our house, watching holiday movies, and the expectancy of the Advent season. I treasure baking Christmas cookies and Amish cinnamon bread and sharing treats with friends—a tradition my kids and I have cherished since they were little. It was a longing that I couldn't explain. But as the days turned to weeks and months, I realized this Christmas would be different.

We were displaced for over nine months. During renovations, nearly everything was replaced—from floors to paint. Just when we thought we were close to returning, disaster struck again. A pipe burst shortly after a new water heater installation, flooding our kitchen and living room, undoing much progress and leaving us heartbroken. Recovery, we learned, is rarely linear.

Through every twist and setback, our faith in God held us steady. Psalm 62:5-6 reminded me that my hope comes from God, that He is my rock and my salvation. When flames threatened our home and uncertainty lingered, we found refuge in God's presence. His strength carried us through sleepless nights and weary days. His hope gave us the courage to face each challenge. Even when plans fell apart, we trusted that His purpose was greater than our pain. Holding onto that hope renewed our spirits and reminded us that no matter how dark the night, His light would always guide us home.

Prayer

Lord, thank you for being our refuge in the storm and our strength when we are weak. Help us to trust You through every challenge, knowing You are always near. Renew our hope and peace, reminding us that Your love will guide us home no matter the trials. Amen.

To Hope for Hope
By Rholyns Mejia

Weeks leading into the submission of this reflection, I've dealt with a multitude of what felt like never-ending chaos – from work deadlines to home life to health, and everything else in between. I looked at the calendar, and it felt like the deadline was drawing nearer and nearer, and nothing was coming to my creative mind. I thought to myself, if I couldn't find time and inspiration to write what would be my first published work in a very long time, then I would just have to let go. Opportunities will come. But then again, what if I run into the same situation? That thought did not bring any relief.

But life has its own ways of nudging us. To me, it was this unplanned sick time I needed to reset my body from the grueling challenges of the days past. I thought to myself, life is too short, and who knows when other opportunities might come along? I looked at the calendar, and it appears I actually had a few more days than I thought. That was hope doing its job.

As soon as I came to realize that I had a little time in my hands, I hoped for the ideas and stories to start throwing words in my head. With a moment of silence, I did something I have not done in a while: pray. I asked for hope to be brought to me, and it came before I even knew it.

As I was looking for inspiration, I came across Romans 8:24-25. I had goosebumps and a chill on my spine when I read it. I thought to myself, life truly has answers to everything, and we just have to ask for it. I did not know if I would have had this idea to write about this day, but this is what I could not see, and therefore hoped for. I waited with patience, but life has been kind, probably knowing that I needed to be saved in such very little time. As if the floodgates had opened their doors, just as quickly the words started to flow. In each word, a stream of hope – hope that I can see flowing to the dry patches of life that needed a little drop to bring forth yearning to live more freely, happily, and thankfully.

I hope that this story sprinkled at least a little bit of what's needed to give you the desire to do what makes you truly happy. If I look at my story as an avenue to reach as many lives as possible to have that spring of motivation and leave them desiring more, I'd be the first person to keep hoping for hope to share and let others give themselves a chance to share their own hope stories in whatever way their hearts choose.

Prayer

Lord, thank you for showing me the things you have set for me, and for letting me see the power of hope in a way I least expected. I will patiently wait for that perfect dose of hope to make me realize what a much better place this life is when we look beyond what our eyes can see. Amen.

The Light That Leads Us Home
By Julie Almodovar

The Christmas during my daughter's first semester of college should have felt comforting. She was home, safe under our roof, where the danger felt contained. But she had been a binge-drinking alcoholic since high school and had recently suffered an alcohol-related head injury. She was having seizures as a result. Relief and fear warred inside me. I was thankful to have her close, yet terrified of what might come next. Christmas didn't feel hopeful—it felt heavy.

Though the house was filled with lights and music, I couldn't rejoice. I'd never felt darkness settle so deeply over a season meant for celebration. One night, after everyone had gone to bed, I sat near the tree watching the lights blur through tears. Those quiet, tree-lit moments had always been peaceful, but now I felt empty and afraid. I whispered, Lord, are You even here?

In that stillness, He moved my heart. I was sitting in the glow of the Christmas tree, because the Light of the World came down to be with us: my daughter, my family, and me. Hope slowly began to rise within me—not from the tree's glow, but from knowing His presence still filled the room and still held my family.

The next day, I read Psalm 36:9 with fresh eyes. God was teaching me to stop looking through a lens of fear and start seeing my daughter—and the unwelcome circumstances—through His light, not the darkness. Only then could I glimpse the hope waiting on the other side.

Advent reminds us that even in the longest nights, the Light is already on its way. It's a season of waiting—not for circumstances to change, but for Christ to come and make all things new. When I stopped staring at the problem and started seeing through His light, everything began to change. I didn't have to fix her. I could just love her. My role wasn't to rescue her; it was to reflect Jesus.

Learning to look through His light took time, but with every small act of faith, He strengthened me. There were plenty of ups and downs yet to come, but He was changing me right in the middle of the storm. Hope grew brighter each time I chose to trust Him instead of letting fear take the lead.

God doesn't just shine His light; He helps you see by it. His light reveals what darkness hides, the evidence of His goodness still at work. It brings order to chaos and clarity to confusion. He isn't a faraway glow but the light that leads you home.

When Jesus was born, Heaven's light broke through earth's night. Angels lit up the sky to announce it—not to kings or scholars, but to shepherds. The Light of the World came quietly to the lowly, not the lofty. Hope slipped into the dark and found the humble, just as it finds you.

And that's what His light still does. In His light, fear loses its power. In His light, the broken begin to heal. In His light, your darkness becomes the very place His glory shines brightest. So lift your eyes. The same Light that was born in Bethlehem still shines for you—steady, radiant, victorious. Even now, as you wait and wonder, that Light draws near. The hope you've been searching for has already come close.

Prayer

Light of the World, thank You for shining into my darkness. When hope feels dim, remind me that Your light never fades. Open my eyes to see through Your light—Your truth in every darkness, Your glory in every moment. Fill me with Your radiant hope so I can reflect it to others. Amen.

Discovering Hope
By Trisha K. Knight

A fire quietly crackles, causing Christmas memories to race through my mind and demand my attention. This Christmas is another one without grandpa, another one far from home. The fire was not even real. We played the fireplace video continuously on a laptop. We dressed the door with a fresh-cut swag, so the smell of pine can fill the room. The pumpkin pies and hot chocolate aromas dance through the air. Peppermint candy canes lie on the table, tempting those who pass by. I clutch the small mug to warm my cold hands. Questions agitate my mind like constant ocean waves. Why so soon? Why, when I'm so far away? Why must things change?

Another shock came that year. I can't remember if it was day or night when I received news of my father's passing. Those days just melted together. I couldn't fly the five thousand miles home to be there for his funeral. I agonized over the two ruptured discs that prevented me from taking the twelve-hour flight. I could only be upright for short moments at a time. I wanted to scream, cry, throw things, break something! The only thing broken that day was my heart.

I often think of others who experience loss during the holiday season. I pray and weep for them as I do for my family. In my twenties, I would have drowned all my emotions in alcohol just to get through. I would have taken drugs to forget. All just to be numb enough, not to care as much. Those days are over! Now, I rely on something else to make it through tough times.

I've learned to reach for God and the hope he brings. Prayer became a necessary staple to me. Throughout the day, I separate from others to pray and cry, then I can keep going. I must move past the pain and hope for a better tomorrow. I talk to God about my concerns. I talk about the pain in my heart, about the unfairness of it all! I listen to the same worship song over and over, until it annoys my roommates! I sit in silence at times, straining to hear God, for him to tell me it will all be okay. And in his way, he does.

Small packages can be very instrumental. One of my beloved nieces was born that Christmas. And later, a second niece was born, her name is Grace. To me, she'll always be "Baby-Grace". Sometimes a little is all we need. I find comfort in God's word. In his promises, He reminds us, when one thing ends, another often begins. New lives, new beginnings, remind me of his promises and peace. Small gifts sometimes take time to grow. God made it so their lives bring hope for a better day.

God sent a child at Christmas to bring out goodness and cause an awakening of rejoicing.

When I get overwhelmed with circumstances that try to steal away what God's given me, I search for new life. It always finds a way to produce hope, peace, and freedom inside me. A child was sent to conquer sin, break bondages, disrupt all pain, transform lives, heal each person, and give hope. God sent his child to bear and endure the cross, so we do not have to. Jesus was sent to bring redemptive life to all people. The holy spirit fills me and causes me to live a life of wholeness, freedom, and gives me enduring hope. As it has been for me, it can be done for you as well.

Prayer

Lord, help us all to find hope in you in the hard times, when it's difficult to see anything. Thank you for the gift of your son. Show your greatness, bring your comfort, and help each one walk in your promises. Let your gift of salvation and hope find each person. Amen.

Hope After Betrayal: When Love Breaks Us

By Lisa Ann Gonzalez

The moment I discovered the truth, the world tilted. All at once. I had loved this person with fierce, unguarded devotion. I defended them when others whispered doubts. I opened my home, my heart, my future to them. In one shattering instant, I learned they had been living a secret—betraying the covenant we had made, then turning it around to blame me. I was the problem. I was too demanding. I was the reason.

Somehow, my heartbreak became my guilt. I looked in the mirror and did not recognize the fool staring back. How could I not have seen? What was wrong with my judgment? I had invested everything—my trust, my vulnerability, my belief in their goodness—and it had all been a mirage. The person I loved most had weaponized the intimacy I had given them.

I spiraled into the darkest question: If God loved me, where was He in this? If He truly loved me, surely,

He would have protected me. Surely His infinite wisdom would have shown me the truth before I poured myself into someone so unworthy. And then I encountered Jesus in a garden at night, knowing exactly what was about to happen.

Jesus sat at a table with twelve men He had chosen and loved deeply. With the clarity of divinity, He knew one of them would hand Him over to be tortured. Another would deny Him three times. All of them would abandon Him in His darkest hour. He loved them anyway.

When He said, "One of you will betray me," did He harden His heart? No. He got on His knees and washed their feet—including the feet of the man who would betray Him. He was not naive. This is someone who sees clearly and chooses to love with shattering clarity anyway.

When Judas arrived in the garden with torches and soldiers, Jesus did not run or demand justice. He looked at his betrayer and said, "Friend." Not with sarcasm. With a voice that held both His full heartbreak and His full grace. I see what you are doing. And I am still here.

The betrayal broke Jesus' heart. His tears in Gethsemane prove it. But it did not destroy His purpose or make Him bitter. Here is what shatters me: Jesus came into this world knowing exactly how it would end. He knew He would be betrayed, denied, abandoned by those He came to save. He came anyway.

You are standing in the wreckage of trust. Someone you loved has weaponized your vulnerability and made you feel guilty for your own heartbreak. You are asking: Where was God?

But listen: Jesus knows what it feels like. He walked this exact road—the devastation of intimacy betrayed, the loneliness of being misunderstood by those closest to Him, the agony of loving someone who uses love against you. He survived it. He transformed it.

The resurrection was not despite the betrayal. It was through it. Jesus walked into devastation and emerged transformed—not hardened, not bitter, but glorified. More loving than before.

Your scars may never fully heal. Your grief is valid. But here is the breathtaking truth: You are not foolish. You are not abandoned in this pain. Your betrayal qualifies you to walk where Jesus walked. If He rose from the deepest betrayal—not destroyed, but resurrected—then transformation is waiting for you too.

Prayer

Jesus, Heal what feels shattered in me—not by making me forget, but by walking with me through it. Restore my capacity to trust, not because the world is safer, but because You are faithful. Resurrect the parts of me that feel dead: my hope, my wholeness, my belief that love is still worth the risk. Amen.

The Getting Well Christmas
By Cara McLauchlan

There is a line of scripture I long to be true in me at Christmas. It's from Luke 2:19 and almost feels like an afterthought. Mary has given birth to Jesus and then pauses to take it all in. After all the travels, barnyard birth, and partying shepherds, this sentence sums up my heartfelt desire for Christmas: " But Mary treasured up all these things, pondering them in her heart" (Luke 2:19).

I'm imagining Mary, glowing in the wonder of her newborn son, resting in lush contentment. She's full of gratitude, cozily taking in the beauty and splendor of all that God has done. I desperately want this to be my mindset every holiday. Cozy, content, grateful, with peace on earth and goodwill to all. For years, I expected to wake up on Christmas morning as treasuring Mary, but instead showed up as the same disappointed me.

Honestly, I thought I needed to work harder. I strategized my holiday to be Mary meets Martha Stewart. Armed with elaborate lists, meaningful Advent studies, beautiful decorations, and curated menus, this would be the "Treasuring Mary" year. Until it wasn't.

Don't get me wrong, I love lists, menus, and ideas for a lovely holiday. But habit stacking my way to the perfect Christmas never worked. Along with all the pretty packages came the same sadness of missing family, relationship worries, gifting insecurities, and guilty spending.

Despite my ridiculous attempts at "managing Christmas," I didn't understand how I could carry so much shame about Jesus's birthday. Why couldn't I treasure like Mary? In my heart, I knew there was only one Mary, and she wasn't me. Something needed to change. Through seasons of prayer and time in the word, I landed on a different scripture. I began to consider John 5:6 instead: "'Do you want to be healed?'"

Jesus speaks these six powerful words to an invalid man who hopes to be magically healed by the waters. For 38 years, he sits by the pool, hoping today is the day. Yet nothing changes. Day after day he keeps doing the same things, expecting big results. Jesus asks him this simple question and it changes everything. Through the healing power of Christ and his decision to believe, the man gets up and walks.

What I'm learning is there are places inside of us that only Christ can heal. No matter our smart attempts at fixing things, brokenness still exists. No amount of striving on my part was going to work. For me, living out the holiday victim story was a trap of my own making, and it was a place that Christ needed to heal.

This Advent season, I'm pressing into this new story. I don't have to live in my own self-decorated prison of pressure, guilt, and shame. I don't always get it right, but Christmas reminds me I can invite Him into the places only He can heal.

What new story is Jesus inviting you to live this Christmas? Whether like me, you struggle with burdens of the past or are excellent at keeping Him the focus, every Christmas is a fresh reminder that Christ was born to bring abundant life for all of us.

He came for all of us to get well. We can pick up our mat, walk, and know it is well with Jesus.

Prayer

Heavenly Father, Show me the new story you want me to tell this Advent. When I start to worry about the details, remind me to choose to be well instead. Slow me down to treasure it all in gratitude. Let your bright star of hope be true this season, this day and every day I am given. Amen.

The One Who Leads Us Home

By Kelly Havemeier

"Mama, where are you?" I cried as I frantically scanned every face in the crowded, bustling mall. It was the height of the Christmas shopping season, and I found myself utterly lost, separated from my mother. I was barely four and desperate to see a familiar face. I searched for anyone wearing the tan, brushed-wool trench coat my mother wore on these chilly days, but to my disappointment, and increasing panic, every fashionable lady wore the same one.

Thankfully, a friendly officer recognized my unfortunate situation, took my hand, and led me back to my mother, stopping only to buy me a lollipop from the candy kiosk on the way. My mother scooped me up, thanked the officer, and held me tight in the safety of her embrace. Our shopping day was done, and it was time to go home—Safe at home with my mother.

This Advent season holds a similar hopeful anticipation of finding the One we most long for, the One who will lead us home. We wait, suspended in wonder for days on end, as this time of year feels extra hopeful and expectant. Whispers of hope are in every little thing, and it has absolutely nothing to do with presents—but Presence.

The prophet, Isaiah, long ago foretold that his name would be Immanuel—God with us. Not behind us or ahead of us, but with us. In only saying the name, Immanuel, God with us, it is a purposeful prayer. Whispered, pleaded, or praised, it is a declaration of hope that the God of the universe is, in fact, with us, even in the silence.

He came as a baby, born of a virgin, leaving heaven to dwell among us. His great love for humanity could not be muted, nor could it ever be. He fulfills our longing for Presence in the most perfect way.

When life feels heavy and everything seems too much to bear, we can remember we need only to call on His name, Immanuel—God with us. We are no longer lost, but merely waiting. We may inhabit a world that is often disordered, yet he is near—with us. He will lead us home.

As a mother and father eagerly await their children to awake Christmas morning and discover the beautiful things left just for them under the Christmas tree, I imagine this is how God must feel. As we wait for Him, He is also waiting with wonderful gifts, all lovely and good, ready to be unwrapped, waiting for His children to awake and come and experience the greatest gift—Presence.

Immanuel is a meeting of God and humanity all in one name. This was the plan all along, even when we could not see it—a design for God to meet us exactly where we are both now and for all of eternity. This is our greatest Hope as we encounter his presence in the holy quiet of Advent and anticipate eternity. He truly is Immanuel—God with us, the One who is with us now and will ultimately lead us home.

Prayer

God, I pray for hope to rise within every heart that has grown weary in the waiting. When breaking news threatens to break hearts, may your presence break through the shadows. You are Immanuel, God with us, both now and forever. All my hope is in you to lead me home to your heart.

Hope in the Waiting

By Tammi Lynn Taylor

"God, I'm done," my fist pounded the steering wheel as bitter fire seared my heart. "If you take this baby, I'm done."

The grocery story parking lot was a conspicuous place to battle the Almighty, but there I sat. Hours before, we had left a prenatal check up with the daunting news that our unborn daughter had genetic issues which could mean many things from inconsequential surgeries to not surviving outside the womb.

Shaken, we prayed on the way home. My parents were with us for Thanksgiving, so we shared with them. We prayed again, then my mom and I drove to get some things from the store. She went in. I stayed in the car and burned with anger.

"Lord, my whole life has been Yours! Since childhood, I have lived for You. We answered the call to ministry and have endured such painful things in obedience.

Must we give up a child now? I can't do it. If you take her, I'm done."

It was beyond childish. It was sinful. When we're desperate we sometimes act like that. I am thankful God is so much bigger than our flesh and our human responses.

All at once, the gravity of God's Presence filled the cabin of my old, gray Suburban like a weighted ball set in my lap. It brought me back from the frantic "what ifs" and felt as though He took my face in His hands.

"Really?" The voice in my heart was consuming fire but also kind. "After all I have done..." My mind began to flood with pictures of all God's goodness in our lives and ministry. The final picture was Jesus, on the cross, conquering death for me. "After all I have done, you couldn't walk this path with Me if I asked you to?"

I broke into heavy sobs, all bitterness gone. Of course. Of course I would walk any path He asked me to. What had He withheld on the path to redeem my soul from death? How many gifts had He given in asking me to partner with Him in Kingdom work? Any pain we had endured was at least equally balanced if not overwhelmed with joy. He deserved all my obedience. He deserved everything. I thought about the gift of my sons at home and surrendered my daughter into His loving arms.

His Presence lifted, but in His wake, He left an overpowering hope. Even if the situation was more than we could handle, He was with us. Even if it meant we only held her for a few hours, He was with us. From that day, I had assurance I could not explain. Fear still tried to take hold. The waiting seemed it would never end. But Jesus was with us.

I wonder if that is how Israel felt as they waited for their Messiah. It is often how I feel as I wait for His return. Paul says it so well in Romans 5: our suffering yields perseverance that yields character that yields hope. That hope won't disappoint us because God's love is poured out in our hearts!

Whatever your circumstance, if you put your hope in God, He can pour His love into your heart and give you greater hope and assurance in His Presence.

Today our little girl is a pre-teen young lady. She embodies hope as she rises like a sunbeam every day and carries the sweet fragrance of Jesus' love wherever she goes. She is a constant reminder that Jesus is worth waiting on, and He is our hope.

Prayer

Jesus, thank You for being my hope. Help me to hope in who You are more than in the outcomes I wish would happen. Give me the assurance of knowing that no matter what comes, You will be with me, and You are everything! I put my desires in Your hands, Jesus, trusting You to lead me in every step.

Hope in the Waiting: When God Whispers Through the Weight

By Jenny Cioto

Have you ever felt the crushing weight of life pressing down so hard it's difficult to even breathe, let alone pray? I have.

I remember sitting at my kitchen table, surrounded by bills, baby bottles, and the noise of five little ones— one of whom we had just adopted to keep a sibling group together. On paper, it looked beautiful. But underneath, I was terrified. We weren't late on a single bill, but every dollar we made was already spoken for. And we swiped credit cards as if they didn't have due dates. We were stuck in a cycle that looked responsible from the outside but was quietly suffocating us on the inside.

My husband was serving in the military, working long hours to provide, and I couldn't bear the thought of adding financial stress to his load. I felt helpless, ashamed, and stuck.

What I didn't know then was that God was already at work—long before I saw any evidence of change.

During Advent, we celebrate the hope of waiting—that sacred stretch of time between promise and fulfillment. The Israelites knew it well, waiting centuries for the Messiah in what must have felt like silence and darkness. I knew it, too, in my own small way, as I waited for a miracle in the middle of unpaid peace and mounting debt.

Then one ordinary morning, when my youngest was just a few months old, God began to whisper. Not audibly, but unmistakably. Everywhere I turned, I saw the words "budget" and "stewardship." My devotional that morning spoke about managing what God entrusts to us. A friend began sharing her story about becoming debt-free and offered to lend me the very books that were helping her.

And for the first time in a long time, I felt it—hope. A flicker of light in the dark.

God was showing me that we weren't alone, that there was a way forward. I realized I had believed a lie—that debt was forever, that financial freedom wasn't for families like ours. But God gently turned my eyes toward His truth. He wasn't just calling me to get out of debt; He was inviting me to trust Him in every area of my life.

That hope changed everything. I confessed my mistakes to the Lord and asked for wisdom. My husband and I began the hard work of stewarding what we had differently—one diaper, one dollar, one decision at a time. It wasn't easy, but three years later, we were completely debt-free.

The same God who met me in my bathroom-floor tears and kitchen-table prayers was faithful. He didn't shame me for my past—He used it to draw me closer.

Maybe this Advent, you're waiting too. Maybe it's not money—it could be healing, reconciliation, or a long-awaited breakthrough. Whatever your darkness looks like, hold on to this truth: the same God who kept His promise to send a Savior is keeping His promises to you.

He hasn't forgotten you. He hasn't left you. Even when you can't see it, He's already at work—whispering hope through His Word, through people, through moments that remind you He's near.

Hope isn't the absence of struggle. Hope is the assurance that God is present in it, faithful through it, and working all things for good.

Prayer

Lord, thank You for being my steady hope in every season of waiting. When I can't see the way forward, remind me that You are already there—making a way. Help me to trust Your timing, rest in Your promises, and see Your light even in the dark. Amen.

Hope Weeps, Too
By Brianna R Wasson

My body needed more sleep, but my brain woke me up before the sun. It had been working to untangle some impossible knots. With Thanksgiving plans in the works, family drama had already started. That meant hard conversations lurked ahead, and it was only October.

Then there was the biopsy, just two days away. If the doctor found nothing, life would move on as usual. Otherwise, I'd be facing some really hard decisions involving scary words with terrifying implications.

Finally, I gave up the ghost and got out of bed. I pressed the coffee and grabbed my journal before I started my daily questions for God. That morning's questions quickly turned desperate. I remembered the story about Lazarus and his sisters, so I turned to John 11 and re-read the narrative. This time, though, my eyes found hope in the two least likely words: Jesus wept.

I found hope in that tiny phrase as I read the story of Jesus' good friend, Lazarus, and his family. Of the grief and suffering they had to endure before the glorious end of the story, when the dead man literally walked himself out of the grave.

When Jesus heard that his friend was sick and needed His healing touch, He decided not to go. The Bible says, in fact, He waited because He loved that family so much. Jesus made the intentional choice not to go and rescue his friend. Instead of preventing suffering, He decided to wait it out. He loved them dearly, so He stayed where He was.

And love like this makes no sense to me.

Jesus knew all along that He was going to raise Lazarus from the dead. So why did He make him suffer? Why did Mary and Martha have to know grief so thoroughly? Why couldn't He let them avoid it? He loved them, so how could He not prevent all that suffering?

When Jesus showed up four days after Lazarus had been buried, though, He stepped into the suffering and experienced it for Himself. Even as He held the plan. He knew His words would bring life and relief.

Even so, He stepped wholeheartedly into the dark and desperate world of mourning and sorrow and grief. He held the hope of Lazarus' resurrection right there in His lungs. And still, Jesus wept.

Hope Himself stepped into the middle of unimaginable grief just as He steps into our stories today. Even when He knew the plan for Lazarus' resurrection, He neither bypassed nor nullified the sisters' sorrow. He entered in and walked grief's path right there with them.

I found such hope in those two words that day. Because the view from the middle of my story was scary and hard, and I wanted to be on the other side of it. But just as Jesus met Martha and Mary in the darkness and terror their brother's death had caused, I knew He would meet me, too.

Because even hope weeps. It doesn't ignore pain. It experiences it right in the middle with us.

I walked into my day and my week confident that Jesus had known such suffering and pain, assured that He felt my mess. I walked in hope because Jesus wept, too.

Prayer

Lord Jesus, thank You for entering our suffering even in the midst. Thank You for the hope that weeps with us. Help us remember this truth today, especially when the mess feels too messy. Amen.

Christmas 1974:
A Glimpse of Heaven
By Traci Jeffrey

I sat looking across our yard, the air full of a quiet magic, and the joy of Christmas bursting from my 10-year-old heart. Time paused to let the snow finish its dance while the sparkle of the night enveloped our home and brought an abundance of joy and the bright promise of morning.

Our whole family arrived that day, arms full of packages, food, and treats. The tree stood at attention in its usual place of honor, twinkling for all to see. The star on top sparkled like a jeweled crown, reminding us of that star long ago.

Presents spilled across the floor in a sea of red and green, and joy filled my heart at the possibilities to come. Christmas 1974 was etched in my memory, not because of the gifts and goodies, but because of the overflowing presence of love and wonder.

More than any surprise, the true gift of that Christmas was the gathering of every family member under one roof. Laughter echoed through our home like the church bells that rang throughout our tiny town. My siblings and I danced and twirled through the night, and though it felt timeless in the moment, that Christmas became the last time our family celebrated the holiday together.

Fragile as a snowflake that melts when touched, life scattered us like pine needles falling on a forest floor. Divorce, distance, and timing pulled us in different directions. The picture and feelings of that night became a photograph frozen in my memory, tucked away to be looked upon at times. What felt like forever that night, in truth, was but a brief moment in time, and yet...

I often return to that faded picture with a longing that is hard to define. Like a stranger in a foreign land, I sometimes find myself adrift and seeking comfort. I return to that place that anchors me to the foundation from which my life flows, and to the promise that was born in a manger long ago. I imagine the love, warmth, and celebration I felt that night was but an earthly glimpse into the heavenly reunion believers will experience one day.

That image became the star I use to navigate trials. It reminds me of our ever-present gift of hope we receive through Christ Jesus and His promise of eternal life. We can rest in the hope that we will one day be reunited with those that we have loved and have gone before us...the sparkling snow becoming the streets of gold, while the food and treats, the feast that will be set at the table prepared for us all.

Hope is a word we can believe in, a reminder of the presence of a living Savior who calls us to him. Hope carries us when life is difficult, and hope in Jesus Christ will lead us home.

As I write these words, my dad is slipping away... his death imminent. I choose to open the album and look upon the photo of that night and remember that warm little house filled with love and joy, and I find peace. I know that in a short time, Dad will rejoice at the greatest family reunion of all. His race well run, his legacy full of love, and his hope fulfilled.

Prayer

Thank you, God, for the gift of the hope of heavenly reunions, for your love for us through your Son, and for life everlasting. Amen

When Heaven Whispered Hope

By Kathleen LaFavre

It was the midst of the Christmas season of 1989, and Advent had always been my favorite time of year. My memories of past Advent seasons were filled with family gatherings, church celebrations, laughter, and the kind of joy that wrapped my heart in warmth. This particular year was feeling strangely different, as one of my favorite people in the world- my grandfather Charlie- had fallen ill once again.

He'd already defied the odds when doctors had given him six months to live, yet he went on to bless his family and friends with nine and a half more years of stories, smiles, and love. This time, his terminal illness felt heavier, and hope for him overcoming the odds did not seem likely to be a reality.

On the evening of December 13, 1989, our family gathered around his bedside. Charlie's breathing began to become labored, as he seemed to be fading in and out of consciousness. His once-radiant smile had faded, and his baby blue eyes would flutter open now and then.

His spirited personality had always consumed a room with storytelling, jokes, and laughter, which was now diminished. The family that surrounded him was sharing their versions of stories and memories of Charlie's well-lived life. It was as if the baton was now being passed from him to his legacy. As we would recap the tales of his life, an occasional gentle squeeze of his hand reassuring us that he was with us, still listening and still offering comfort in his final moments.

There was a presence of peace that filled the room that evening, and an unexplainable comfort that the family was all experiencing. It was the kind of peace that reassured us that God's presence was among us and the hope of knowing that Charlie was about to transition to his heavenly home. We clung to Romans 5:5, knowing that hope does not disappoint.

We were not ready to let Charlie go, but we all gained comfort knowing of his assurance of heaven. Charlie lived a life on this earth that was full, rich in relationships, a true overcomer of challenges, and impactful to all those he encountered. He was not an overly religious man; however, the conduct of how he treated everyone he encountered, as if they were valued and his friend, left such an impact on me as a young adult. His life was a beautiful example of loving others and spreading joy.

As his breathing slowed, Charlie took one last deep breath at 10:12 pm and left his earthly body. As the breath left his body, the voice of Bing Crosby singing "Silent Night" came across the radio. No one in the room remembered or realized the radio was on until that very moment. It truly felt like one last wink from Charlie as he departed this earth on his way to heaven. There was such an angelic presence that filled the room.

As a twenty-year-old witnessing that sacred transition, I knew that this moment reassured me of a hope I had in Christ. The hope of knowing that a life well lived on this earth and transitioning into a heavenly home with our Lord and Savior has continued to give me peace and comfort. That Advent season became the most monumental and hope-filled in shaping my life, because I truly saw God's faithfulness even in loss.

Prayer

Lord, in this holy season of waiting, remind us that hope is not lost in sorrow but reborn through Your promise of eternal life. As light pierced the night in Bethlehem, may Your light pierce our hearts today–renewing peace, comforting grief, and filling us with steadfast hope in You. Amen.

Our First Christmas Came With Hope

By Melinda R Savage

The first year Jerry and I were married, we lived far from our families. Jerry was in the US Army, and we were stationed in West Germany. We faced many adjustments that year—being far from home, learning a new language and customs, and figuring out military ways, while expecting our first child.

It was comforting as Christmas approached that Germany's winter climate reminded me of home, with snow but not a lot of freezing temperatures. Growing up, we always had an artificial Christmas tree because my mom was allergic to evergreens. No matter the weather, we'd decorate the tree a week before Christmas, on my brother's birthday, singing carols while trimming the tree, then celebrating with cake, ice cream, and gifts. Christmas Eve was just as special, it was my mom's birthday, and we'd read from the Bible about Jesus' birth, celebrating both her life and His.

That first Christmas in Germany, we wanted it to be meaningful. We invited a single serviceman from the church to spend the holiday with us. We had our Christmas stockings, but so he wouldn't feel left out, I made him a stocking from red and green felt. Christmas stockings are fun to see what candy and gifts are inside.

We ordered our tree through the mail, and it arrived just in time. It stood only eighteen inches tall, plastic, but charming with tiny lights and ornaments. A shopping trip to a store called "Christkindlmarkt" (the literal translation is the Christ Child Market), was filled with handmade Christmas decorations. This lifted our spirits and made us feel hopeful.

One December evening, all the ladies from church were invited to a Christmas party at our bishop's home. The sweet fragrances and music filled the air. My friend Tammy and I sat admiring the beautiful tree when she quietly confided that they wouldn't have a tree that year. Her husband's pay had been cut, and money was tight. Tammy tried to make it sound like it didn't bother her, saying her children were too young to notice, but I could hear the sadness in her voice.

That night, I told Jerry what she'd said. By this time, Christmas was only a few days away. We went to the post exchange (PX) the next day to find that the only Christmas tree left was the one on display, already strung with lights.

The store clerk sold us the Christmas tree for just a few dollars. We also got a couple of toys for Tammy's children. Jerry mentioned their situation to our bishop, who helped get groceries for the family, which we picked up on our way home.

Two days before Christmas, with frost still in the air, we loaded our car and drove to Tammy's apartment building. We found their home on the third floor. Quietly, we arranged the box of food, the Christmas tree, and presents outside their door. Once everything was in place, I hurried downstairs while Jerry waited to ring the doorbell. As soon as he did, he quickly came down the stairs, then we raced to the car, hoping not to get caught.

Tammy told me, a while later, how that surprise had changed her perspective. Hearing her words touched me deeply. What had begun as a difficult Christmas became a reminder of hope and love. This small act of kindness changed our perspective, too. From then on, we looked for opportunities to bring hope to others, especially during Christmas.

Prayer

Heavenly Father,

I'm grateful for this opportunity to share this story of hope that I have carried in my heart for a very long time. I hope it can inspire others to look beyond despair and find hope, whatever the circumstances are. In the name of Jesus Christ, Amen.

WINTERING

By Kananileialoha Kawika

In the season of Advent,
the apple tree lies dormant.
Her branches barren and bowed,
heavy, with snow; Her song, silent.

As she rests, her curled fingers
house icicles instead of apples,
and her leafless boughs stretch
stunted limbs skyward.

I wonder, when she sleeps,
does she dream of Winter's end?
Or after weeks of night, has she
forgotten the taste of summer.

This I know: As deep as the frost,
her roots have travelled, waiting,
longing for the chance to bear fruit;
Never doubting the return of Spring.

Prayer

Lord,

Just as the apple tree rests her roots beneath the snow, may you lead us, your people, towards rest and restoration this season. Despite the weight of whatever sorrows we may carry, teach us to welcome well the sacred rhythm that winter brings. May we encounter daily the beauty of your presence, as we step into the waiting and wonderment of Advent, anticipating the birth of Hope. Amen.

Reflections on Peace

Peace be with You

By Janet Bryant Brown

As I sat on the bed with the news that I was pregnant again, holding my five-month-old baby girl in my arms, tears coursed down my face. How could I endure another pregnancy so soon and care for two babies at once? Our tiny efficiency apartment and limited funds only added to my overwhelm.

The conditions weren't ideal—much like Mary's, the mother of Jesus, who journeyed while heavily pregnant on a dusty, uncomfortable donkey, only to be turned away from the inn. I imagined her wondering how she ended up in such humble conditions—giving birth on a dirt-covered barn floor, surrounded by all manner of farm animals—when the time came to deliver the Messiah. I believe she reminded herself that the angel Gabriel spoke peace upon her.

Mary had the divine assurance that she was chosen to carry the Prince of Peace, and that must have calmed her heart in the midst of imperfect circumstances. Peace flooded that space—not because the setting was serene, but because Jesus was there. As Mary wrapped the babe in swaddling cloths, He wrapped her in peace with His Presence.

I thought about my own humble circumstances and how I, too, was chosen by God to carry a child according to His purpose. I chose to hold tightly to the same words the angel Gabriel spoke to Mary, and peace settled in my heart, assuring me that everything was going to be okay.

It was a peace I couldn't explain. It was more than a feeling—it was a sacred connection with the Prince of Peace in my imperfect situation. He is our peace, our clarity, our confidence—not because life is perfect, but because He is.

Peace is the place we all long to dwell, no matter our circumstances. It brings hope, joy, grace, and the quiet confidence that everything will be okay. Though difficult to define, peace is unmistakable when it settles in our hearts and harmonizes with our spirits.

Peace is more than a feeling. It's a connection—a divine bridge built when God removed the barrier between us by sending Jesus as a baby, born through Mary's earthly vessel.

I named my daughter Mary after Jesus' mother to remind me how God chose the Prince of Peace to dwell in our hearts, wrapping us in everlasting peace.

When our peace feels shaken, we can remember that it came wrapped in swaddling cloths—ushering in a relationship with God. A love that meets us in every moment. A hope that shines in every situation. A peace that transcends understanding and can never be taken away.

We may not always feel peace, but we can seek it, pursue it, and lean into it at any time. We can remember who Peace is. We can embrace peace through prayer, scripture, worship, and by remembering that God sent the Prince of Peace into our hearts through a baby in a manger— born into imperfect circumstances so we can know He is with us in our own less-than-perfect moments.

If your peace feels unsettled, invite the Prince of Peace to wrap you in His Presence and calm your heart. True peace begins with connection—with God Himself. When you draw near to Him, you'll discover a peace that goes beyond circumstances, a peace that anchors your soul.

Prayer

Prince of Peace,

Thank you for being near, even when life feels anything but peaceful. In the chaos, confusion, and quiet longings of our hearts, You remain steady—our calm, our assurance. Help us to remember that peace is not found in perfect circumstances, but in Your Perfect Presence. Amen

The Gift of Peace
By C.K. Tuttle

Christmas, one of the most chaotic and stressful times of the year, yet one of the most important celebrations we hold as Christians. Jesus' birth was chaotic; He was born in a barn, surrounded by animals. Can you imagine Mary's heart? Do you think it was calm?

I remember the birth of my firstborn- my precious son. We went to church that Sunday morning, my water broke that afternoon, and we checked into the hospital that evening. Unfortunately, things didn't progress on their own, but luckily my doctor knew just what to do. By Monday afternoon, our bundle of joy had made his entrance into the world. The night had been long, and the waiting seemed to take forever, but God delivered the perfect gift in His perfect timing. All was calm in the hospital room after my son's birth. His aunts, uncles, and grandparents surrounded us and wrapped us in love. The newness of life that I held in my arms quickly reminded me of the newness of life we have in Jesus.

Have you ever wondered why we sing the lyrics that we sing at Christmas time? Was everything truly "calm and bright" at the manger scene? Did Jesus really bring "peace on earth" when He was born? I believe the answer is a resounding "yes!"

Join me on a quick adventure as we discover how the Messiah brought peace into the world. In the Old Testament, Jesus' birth was foretold, and He was given many titles in Isaiah 26:3. One of those titles was "Prince of Peace." In the gospels of Matthew, Mark, Luke, and John, Jesus' life and teachings encourage us to live in harmony with others. He said, "Blessed are the peacemakers." (Matt. 5:9) In His death, he conquered sin so that we could find peace in knowing we have eternal life with him.

You see, peace is not something we can grab ahold of on our own. What do you think Mary did in those moments of stress as she was traveling on a donkey, fully pregnant, only to show up and not have a room to give birth? I will tell you what I would've been doing: praying. I would have been asking the Lord to calm my heart.

This Christmas season, take moments to pause. Be still. Pray for peace. Allow the Holy Spirit to gift you with the "peace of God, which surpasses all understanding" (Philippians 4:7). Just like any parent, God finds joy in giving His children the gifts they ask for. This season, I challenge you to simply ask for peace.

Prayer

Heavenly Father, this Christmas season, we thank You for the gift of Peace. Thank you for sending your Son to bring peace into our world, teaching us how to abide in You and find peace through prayer. We ask that You help us become peacemakers in our community, showing kindness to strangers and shining Your light and love to all.

The Gift You Already Have
By Hannah Louise Cox

Today, everything in the world and in my own relationships feels heavy, and I feel the weight on my heart and my mind. At the same time, how I feel right now isn't unique to this moment or even this year. We are not alone in our craving for peace.

The Christmas season has a way of stirring the pot, as it invites us to return to the reason for this season. Trusting Jesus.

I have memories of a handful of Christmases that were peaceful, and they are beautiful memories. The majority of my memories are filled with relatives arguing over politics that somehow got brought up, fighting over why that one relative doesn't show up more throughout the year, and petty competitions over who made the better dish or dessert.

I have no idea how your Christmas will look or how you are feeling this year. Perhaps you can't relate to my ghosts of Christmas past, but if I know anything about the human spirit, we crave peace. We want the chaos of our inner and outer world to calm down. We want our table to be calm, our conversations peaceful and not shallow, and our angst to come to a simmer.

The good news is that in Christ we have peace. He gave it to us. We possess peace through His Spirit inside of us. We have it, but I think, like many good things in our lives, we forget that we do. So, if the Prince of Peace gave us His peace, then how do we access it?

Jesus doesn't give like we do. Peace isn't a result of our circumstances changing, families behaving, and the world calming down. Peace comes from believing and trusting that Jesus is who He claims to be.

Trust Jesus with your heart. Trust Jesus with your family. Trust Jesus with your community. Trust Jesus with your church. Trust Jesus with your country. Trust Jesus with every leader. Trust Jesus with our world. Trust Jesus with your Christmas. Give every fear, worry, want, and desire to Him, and no matter how this season or the next plays out, you'll feel His peace with you, no matter the circumstances.

A few Christmases back, it was my family's first Christmas without my dad's parents and only a few months after my Nana died. To say I wasn't looking forward to my first Christmas without her would be an understatement. I was dreading it. How could we do Christmas without the heart of our families' holiday?

However, there was a sense of peace surrounding the holiday. Even though it was messy and far from easy, that Christmas was filled with God's peace. It wasn't a perfect Christmas, but choosing to trust Jesus with my broken heart and every care I had made that Christmas and season of grief and family turmoil, peace filled because I knew Jesus cared about my family, our loss, and how it was all affecting me.

Jesus cares about you and everything that is filling you with unease right now. Your circumstances may not change or improve this Christmas. Your family will still show up with the same energy they always have. Your kids may still struggle with the "I want" monster. You may still be waiting for an answer to your prayers. The world may indeed still feel like a dumpster fire. But I promise you, because Jesus promised us that His peace has been given to you, in the midst of every circumstance, you have His peace.

Trust Jesus and experience the gift of peace He's given you.

Prayer

Jesus, thank you for the gift of peace that You have given us. Help us to trust You with every care that occupies our hearts and minds, and for how it all works together for our ultimate good and Your glory. May Your peace be felt in our hearts and lives, no matter the circumstances. Amen.

Because He Came – Everything Changed

By Jerralea Miller

What if I told you that because a certain baby was born, you can have a fresh start, a do-over, with a clean slate? You could become a new person in God's eyes with all mistakes blotted out. Your sin-darkened form would become as white as snow when He looks at you.

When Angel Gabriel announced to Mary that she would give birth to Jesus, he told her Jesus would be called the Son of God, given the throne of David, and his kingdom would never end. Mary's people, the Jews, believed God would send a Messiah who would rescue them politically. She never could have imagined how privileged she was to participate in a birth that would affect worship and solve the problem of sin.

When Christ came, everything changed. Before Christ, a priest had to make a sacrifice once per year for the people's sins (Exodus 30:10). Christ came and offered himself as a sacrifice for our sin, once for all time (Hebrews 10:10) Before Christ, prayer was not an open communication among all (Daniel 6:10). After Christ, we, ourselves, can approach God whenever we are in need (Hebrews 4:16). Before Christ, a sin offering could be made only at the temple (Deuteronomy 12:5-7).

After He came, we can approach the throne room of God any time, any place, as we live our daily lives (Ephesians 6:18). Because He came, He understands us. He lived life with us in the humblest of circumstances. He knows how it is to be human (Hebrews 4:15).

Now, we can have peace with God. We can make things right with God anytime, anywhere. But that's not all! Believers can look to the future with confidence. Jesus promised He is preparing a place for us, and He will come back and get us, so we will always be where He is (John 14:2-3).

His first coming brought peace between God and man. His second coming will usher in an eternity of peace in a Home with Him.

Prayer

Abba,

We're thankful Jesus came as a baby to grow, live among us, and experience our humanity. He understands us! But it didn't stop there: He went to the cross, redeeming us from sin. Now, we're viewed through the lens of the righteousness of Jesus. Because He came, everything changed.

We're beyond grateful. In Jesus' holy name we pray, amen.

Peace in Every Season

By Joy Caswell

As we celebrate the second week of Advent, we light the candle for Peace. Advent peace is a season of God ruling in our hearts and actions. His peace calms our anxieties, restores our relationships, and anchors us with hope when life feels unsettled, much like the peaceful silence on a cold, snowy day. The snow blankets everything with a fresh new perspective.

In Colossians, Paul reminds us that Christ's peace must rule in our hearts so that we can decide how we respond to worry, fear, or conflict. Instead of letting our circumstances or emotions control us, we are called to let his peace guide us. Peace during Advent is a reconciliation with God that leaves us feeling complete and whole.

Think back to the lessons from the birth of Jesus, who was born in a barn and then placed in a manger. He didn't have a nice bedroom with the perfect theme painted on his bedroom wall. Mary, Joseph, and Jesus simply stayed long enough for them to rest before continuing their journey.

Jesus entered the world amid political unrest, poverty, and fear, yet the angels proclaimed peace on earth. Furthermore, the shepherds, the angels, and the kings all knew where to find him. True peace doesn't depend on circumstances, but in Christ alone. Do not let this world take you captive through its philosophy and deception; instead, turn your eyes and heart to God, and let him guide your every step.

God and scripture are your navigation in this world; together, they help you clearly find the road you need to be on. Scripture is the primary way God speaks to us, and how he shows us where our boundaries are, so we don't slip and fall. The enemy knows the word of God, too; he will often twist the truth out of context and rob you of your peace. This is how all the emotional stress builds up in your life. Scripture will always validate God's message to you, whether you're looking for direction or trying to navigate through life lessons.

Reset your heart and mind during this Advent season. Let God be the focus of your heart and mind. Turn your focus toward things above. Do not cling to the material things of this world; they will only distract you from the true meaning of the season. Start a new tradition this Advent season. When you arrive at your destinations, take a few photos, then put the devices away and enjoy the moments you have together with friends and family. This time is precious and will help you find peace within every moment. Remember, it is not about how we look, what we have under a tree, or how many decorations we have; it is about having peace in your heart that only God can bring.

Prayer

Gracious Heavenly Father,

Thank you for stepping into our broken world with your calming presence. Fill our hearts with peace that only you can bring. Help us to trust you when we are anxious and share your peace with others. Lord, please heal our broken world. Show us the reason for this Advent season through hope, peace, love, and joy

Rejoice! Peace Has Come

By Linda J. Dingeldein

Laying down His glory, disrobed of His majesty, He came. Redemption's love beating in His heart of flesh. Son of man. Son of God. Immanuel. God has come to dwell with us. Deity born in humility. Divinity with skin. Peace has come!

He came to a world filled with broken hearts and weary souls. Sin, hatred, and rampant strife filled the earth. The calm of "silent night, holy night" was shattered!

Peace is not the absence of struggle. It coexists with weariness and fear, permeating the tumultuous soil of our anxious hearts, mysteriously sweeping over us as soon as we acknowledge the Peace-Giver.

A heavy foreboding crashed over me as the miles took us farther away from home.

Now, as we sat in the parking garage of the Cleveland Clinic, I felt an urgency to stop and pray. We had been praying, but somehow this appointment felt different. Deep inside, I sensed we were embarking on a life-altering journey.

I removed my seatbelt and turned to face my husband. "I feel like God is asking if we are willing to trust Him, even before we know the outcome." My voice cracked as my eyes filled with unshed tears. "I don't want to waste this opportunity for God to be glorified."

I would not realize until later that as my husband and I joined hands to pray, this parking garage prayer would mark a significant moment for both of us. It would become a key reminder that God Himself is our peace, even in the face of uncertainty.

A week later, I received the diagnosis, B-cell Non-Hodgkin Lymphoma. Clearly not the one we had hoped for.

How grateful I was that God prompted me to pray before the diagnosis and draining treatments that followed. It was paramount for me to choose peace before I was hit with painful reactions, sleepless nights, and questions about my future. God knew I would need to look back on our prayer to get me through the difficult days ahead.

As friends followed my cancer journey on social media, some would question me. "Do you actually feel God's peace, or are you just putting on a brave face?"

Immediately, I felt like my faith was being challenged. I desperately wanted God to be glorified. So, I answered with astounding assuredness, "God has mysteriously infused His peace in me during these painful and uncertain days of cancer. He has filled me with something so supernatural that I can't even begin to grasp it. Trust me. It's real!"

Later, I would write these words in my journal: "I don't know what this means, but I do know that God is God, and He is worthy to be praised and trusted. I want him to be glorified through my life. And if it is His will, my death."

Peace comes as we remember who God is and reflect on what He has done. In the midst of adversity, God leads us into peace with purpose, even when we don't see a way forward, backward or in between. Incomprehensible peace enters our hearts as we look to Christ, the Peace-Giver.

Prayer

Jesus, you came that holy night to capture my heart. Your love story is one of redemption, a divine invitation to exchange my struggle for your peace. During this holy season, help my heart to join the host of heaven in worship, singing, "Glory to God in the highest, and on earth peace among those with whom he is pleased!" (Luke 2:14) Amen.

When Peace takes the Place of Perfect

By Jenn Landry

I've always longed for a Hallmark movie kind of Christmas: warm, comforting, aesthetically pleasing, if not slightly predictable. Falling in love with a down-to-earth local dressed in plaid, uniting a community for a common cause, wrapping up in a romantic kiss after the cookie contest set in front of a pristinely lit Christmas tree. It just sounds so perfect and peaceful.

But Christmases like that don't exist in real life, at least not in mine. I live in a big city, not a cute small town. I've never fallen in love, the cookies are unfortunately always undercooked despite my best efforts, and the lights and ornaments on the tree never quite match my imaginative, Pinterest-inspired vision.

The reality of Christmas is a scratched and ring-stained table, too large for a dwindling, never-expanding family. The corner where grandparents once sat is empty. Many of the aunts, uncles, and cousins don't make it down for the holidays anymore. And in my mind, there is a seat still saved for the husband who has yet to show up and places for children who never arrived, next to my aging parents.

It can feel painfully disappointing to face the holiday letdown each year. Christmas can vividly illuminate the void of a life I thought I would have by now.

It is easy to lament, but when I take the time to peel back the layers of my disappointment juxtaposed with the true meaning of the Christmas season, I inevitably uncover something way more special than a Hallmark story.

Reading the gospel of John reminds me that peace isn't dependent on a picture-perfect fantasy. Instead, it is wholly shaped by the Prince of Peace. Jesus's words consistently highlight a peace that surpasses my meager human understanding. Jesus's brand of peace isn't cleverly masquerading behind a beautiful exterior but rather a raw invitation to lean on Him for strength that is meant to prevent our hearts from being troubled.

This steady peace pulses underneath the pursuit of a perfect Christmas if I am paying attention. Even though the fiction of a Hallmark Christmas Movie faithfully appears on my TV screen each year in perhaps too many variations, the true meaning of Christmas announces itself in a much more convincing way. Edging out the weight of the disappointment of a present that doesn't match what I'd hoped for.

His peace protects my tender heart and soothes the weariness of waiting when I revisit the kind ways He encounters humanity. Always with grace and goodness. And if that isn't the greatest romance I could ever know—truly better than any narrative a Hallmark movie could craft.

Prayer

Jesus, let peace flow like a thick current through the disappointment and unfulfilled dreams exacerbated by a celebratory season. May your perfect peace buoy our souls above our lament and longing. May this year's Christmas be an invitation to pause and experience who You are as our Prince of Peace with greater intimacy than we have ever experienced before.

Peace in the Pause

By Angie Hanson

The world around me was loud—so loud that even my thoughts felt like they were shouting. It was the first December after everything in my life had changed. The season that once sparkled with excitement now pressed heavily on my chest. Everyone else seemed to be rushing toward joy—decorating trees, baking cookies, wrapping gifts—but I was just trying to breathe.

One morning, I sat at my kitchen table, coffee growing cold in my hands. The to-do list stared at me, and grief hovered close, whispering reminders of what I'd lost. I remember asking God, "How do I find peace when everything feels so broken?"

That's when it happened—not a booming revelation, but a soft stillness that filled the room. It wasn't that my pain disappeared, but in that pause, I felt a gentle knowing deep in my spirit: I am with you. It was God's peace—quiet, steady, and completely out of place in the chaos.

Philippians 4:7 says, "And the peace of God, which surpasses all understanding, will guard your hearts and your minds in Christ Jesus." I used to read that verse and wonder how peace could possibly "guard" anything. But that morning, I understood. His peace didn't fix my circumstances—it protected my heart from the noise of the world. It was a shield of stillness, reminding me that even when life felt unsteady, He was not.

During Advent, we wait for the coming of Christ—the Prince of Peace. Yet waiting doesn't mean doing nothing. It's a sacred pause. A deep breath. A moment to remember that peace isn't found in perfect days, but in His perfect presence.

I began to notice that peace isn't always loud or obvious. Sometimes it shows up in the slow rhythm of candlelight flickering against the dark. In a quiet prayer whispered through tears. In the gentle nudge to put the phone down, silence the world, and listen for God's still, small voice.

Each time I choose to pause, I feel His peace meet me again. Not because I've earned it, but because He's already here—steady in the storm, calm in the chaos.

Maybe you're reading this and your world feels loud, too. The holiday season can stir up both joy and ache. But peace isn't the absence of pain—it's the presence of Jesus in it. So take a deep breath. Light a candle. Let the noise fall away for just a moment.

Because sometimes, the holiest thing we can do is pause. And in that pause, we discover that His peace was never out of reach—it was waiting quietly for us to notice.

Prayer

Lord, quiet my restless heart. When the world feels loud and heavy, help me find You in the pause. Teach me to rest in Your steady presence and to trust that Your peace is always near—unshaken, unchanging, and enough for today. Amen.

Light Will Shine in the Darkness

By Linda Rose

Lights twinkle, blink, flash, and sync with holiday music, illuminating the night, broadcasting cheer (and sales of holiday must-haves), vying for our attention. At the close of the day, however, a plug is pulled or a switch is flipped, and they are extinguished. It is dark again.

Darkness has been my uninvited companion since childhood. The depression that randomly settles upon my heart and mind particularly intensifies as the Christmas season approaches. Whether sourced from family dynamics, genes, or winter-gray days, the goal of the enemy of my soul is to steal the joy and peace that seem to be everyone else's experience.

Perhaps you know someone who struggles similarly. Perhaps they don't share that, and you would never guess. Maybe it's silently you.

The intent to rob all that is good stands in sharp contrast to Jesus' promise of overflowing life in abundance (John 10:10). A promise that would dispel the grayness. Sent via a billboard intervention or sky-written note addressed to me... not likely, of course, but earnestly needed.

How could a believer be smothered in fog while knowing the profound meaning of this season of celebration, hope, and peace?

Rather than a billboard message, familiar Christmas Scripture passages came to mind – so familiar that many of us can recite them by rote. While this is good, the deeper meaning can be missed in the recitation. Here and now, I longed for the wonder inscribed there to write a new understanding on my heart.

The Father loves to read to His children. To show us new insights into His timeless truth and unwrap the layers of the familiar to reveal exactly what we need in the present moment. To make a personal application from His living Word to our seeking souls.

He didn't write a message in the sky; at least not via aircraft condensation trails. Far superior, the Father's written Word reminded me that He used the whole of His heavens as a show-and-tell canvas to proclaim the answer to our darkness.

Jesus came as a baby in the blackness of night – not on a sunny day. It was shadowed and ordinary until a brilliant angel host blinded shepherds on their common hillsides. The heavenly beings' arrival would have been sufficiently miraculous. But the Father made sure no one missed His gift by settling a huge star over the humble nursery. A giant nightlight that showed the way to the Way. A floodlight that beckoned the waiting weary to come and see.

Light shining upon people walking in darkness (Isaiah 9:2) is a frequent theme in Scripture. Our Father knows that without Him, "walking in darkness" is our experience. Light that cannot be extinguished - peace beyond human understanding - that's what we need. That's what He delivers - but never according to protocol. His outrageous response to our darkness was to deliver His Son and call Him the Light of the world. By following Him, we have the light of life (John 8:12).

When we can't see physically, the light of even a small candle causes shadows to retreat. The same is true for the anguish of the soul: The entrance of His light reveals truth against the looming lies hidden by darkness. Like a lighthouse, our Father stands guard over our hearts and minds with His peace (Philippians 4:7).

When darkness threatens to blot out the peace and promise of the season, recall that brilliant star positioned above the earthly birthplace of the Prince of Peace. The One who was not only born but died and rose again for us. The answer to our longings.

Prayer

Father, may the one reading the words offered here experience Your light breaking through any darkness of heart, mind or soul that threatens to steal peace and joy from the celebration of this miraculous season. May this one truly know You as the Prince of Peace and Light of the world.

Wrestling to Rest

By Tammi Lynn Taylor

The tiny girl wriggled and writhed in my arms. It was obvious every cell within her needed sleep, but she wanted nothing of it. Exhaustion would pull her toward relaxation, but her body would suddenly stiffen as she fought against surrender. Heavy eyelids fluttered to close, but before feathery lashes could touch her cheeks, they would snap open again, raging against rest.

I cooed, lightly jostled, and coaxed her with soft melodies. That had worked for her brothers. She, however, was unconvinced. Sleep wasted precious time she needed to engage her world. Though she was so little, though her body begged her desperately, her mind refused the blissful necessity of restorative peace. Eventually, she could fight no longer, and she fell hard into deep sleep.

It seems obvious to us, doesn't it? Rest is good. Peace feeds abundant life. Yet, in the face of my own battles for safety and control, I'm often no better than my sweet, infant daughter was.

I writhe. I wrestle.

Jesus whispers, "I am your Shepherd; I have everything you need."

I nod, then wring my hands and pace the floor again.

"Do not let your heart be troubled; cast your cares upon me," the Spirit soothes.

I breathe deep, agree for a moment, then fall back into frantic efforts against unknown outcomes, seeking a comfort of my own choosing.

I'm so thankful my Savior knows how to lead me beside quiet waters, even if I wrestle along the way. Isn't it good to know that He understands our humanity? He is compassionate and gracious, slow to anger and abounding in love (Psalm 103:8).

We desire peace to come neatly packaged in solved problems and comfortable circumstances. True peace, though, is not connected to our situation. True peace is fully tied to who our Savior is and the assurance of our place with Him.

The peace of Jesus never revolved around His situation. Remember the boat in the storm? He was at rest, though the Disciples feared death. He, completely unfazed by the waves, spoke the storm to stillness. Our comfort doesn't define peace. He is our peace.

Jesus' entrance into the world was amidst upheaval. His people were under Roman rule. His paternity seemed questionable. His parents were far from home. There was no perfectly-painted nursery waiting– only a manger and some animals to bear witness.

Jesus' coming was not a huge celebration with extended family to dote over Him. Instead, He was lauded by shepherds – a flock of strangers. Despite the Christmas songs... it was likely not a "silent night." It was to this disarray God the Father chose to send His Promise of Redemption: our Prince of Peace.

He came to bring order to our chaos. Wholeness to our brokenness. Calm to our frantic. He is peace in the midst, not in spite of the trouble. His peace surpasses understanding, and it is everything we desire.

Will we receive Him? Can we surrender to His heart and allow Him to speak calm to our souls, even as the storm rages all around us? He is able. Pray with me.

Prayer

Jesus, my Prince of Peace. I invite you into the chaos around me. I believe that You can bring peace in my upheaval. I agree with what You say is true. Please enter my frantic space, Jesus, and bring Your peace beyond understanding. Teach me to stop wrestling and help me simply rest in You. In Your Name, Jesus. Amen.

Calvary's Playbook for Peace

By Kimberly Pearson

"You don't want peace. You want vindication." The Holy Spirit's words hit me mid-argument, my finger pointed, my voice raised, mentally cataloging every wrong he'd committed since 2011.

It was true. I wanted him to admit he was wrong, to feel the weight of what he'd done, to pay for the pain he'd caused me. But God had other plans. He was about to show me what real peace costs and who pays for it.

That burning need for justice: I know it well. The world says peace comes through strength, and they're not wrong. They just misunderstand what kind of strength it takes. God's strategy isn't about scoring points; it's about absorbing hits. This isn't a defensive play; it's taking the penalty for the other team.

It reminds me of Isaiah's prophecy about the Suffering Servant in Isaiah 53:4-5: "Surely he has borne our griefs and carried our sorrows... upon him was the chastisement that brought us peace, and with his wounds we are healed." Notice the transaction: He has borne—He carried—He suffered—upon Him was the chastisement. We receive peace. That's not partnership. That's substitution. That's the gospel.

God made peace with man by the blood of His Cross. He didn't sidestep our sin; He bore the penalty for it completely. Love doesn't merely avoid creating costs for others; love suffers on behalf of others. This terrifies us, doesn't it? Every fiber of our being screams for justice. Yet Christ calls us to lay down our right to retribution.

But here's what God's way does: when we stop demanding payment, we become untouchable in ways that matter. They may attack our reputation, but not our identity. They can wound our feelings but not our foundation. They can steal our comfort but not our calling. They can't take what we've already chosen to give. When we live this way – choosing to absorb rather than retaliate – our sacrifice mirrors His, and the gospel becomes tangible. We put Christ on display by running His plays, not ours.

Calvary teaches us that peace is not a feeling to achieve; it's a price to pay. This is what Calvary looks like on ordinary Tuesdays. It's the wife who stops keeping score in her marriage, who chooses to say "I love you" first after a fight, who prepares his favorite dinner after harsh words, who prays for him when she'd rather bash him. It's the employee who responds to unfair criticism with grace, takes notes during the unjust review, asks how they can improve, and blesses the boss who belittles them. It's the parent who absorbs their teenager's anger without retaliating, who stands firm when doors slam, who whispers prayers when accusations fly, who keeps showing up with lunch money and love notes despite the rolled eyes. Each act of absorption becomes a miniature portrait of the gospel, another play from Calvary's playbook. The question isn't whether you have the power to make them pay; it's whether you dare to pay for them.

You're not strong enough, and neither am I. But Christ in us? That's a different story. The Cross isn't just the place where we obtain salvation and peace with God; it's our blueprint for peace with man.

Prayer

LORD, You see the face in my mind and know what they've done. This Advent, remind me that the Prince of Peace came quietly, vulnerably, taking on sin and injustice. As I wait for His second coming, help me absorb wrongs, show grace, and choose peace, reflecting Your sacrifice in my daily life. In Jesus's name, Amen.

Wrapped in Peace: His Calm in Chaos
By Julie Almodovar

When Operation Desert Storm began, my husband, Dave, was deployed to Saudi Arabia. We'd married that Christmas Day, less than two weeks earlier, in front of my parents' Christmas tree—candles glowing, snow falling, joy mingled with fear. I was both a third-grade teacher and music teacher by day, but became a news consumer by night, desperate for reassurance he was safe.

One Monday afternoon on my way home from work, the radio cut in with breaking news: a Scud missile had struck a building housing American soldiers. The description matched exactly where Dave was stationed. I shot up a quick prayer as my heart pounded, tears blurred the road, and panic rose like a wave—until something holy interrupted it.

A warmth enveloped me like a thick blanket. A calm I had never experienced and couldn't explain filled me. I even tried to make myself worry again, but I couldn't.

Fear had simply lost its grip, and peace wouldn't let go. Later that night, I learned Dave was safe. Relief washed over me, but I already knew he was fine. The real miracle had already come.

Peace isn't a feeling we create; it's a Person who comes close. Scripture says when we turn our fears into prayers, God's peace guards our hearts and minds beyond understanding. (Philippians 4:6-7) That's exactly what I experienced—Jesus Himself covered my panic and filled my heart.

In that moment, I caught a glimpse of the peace our weary world longed for—the peace that first entered humanity's chaos in Bethlehem. Advent reminds us that the same Savior who was born to bring peace still enters our stories today, steadying trembling hearts and quieting our fears. The peace promised to shepherds on a hillside didn't come through politics or power—it came as a Person, the Prince of Peace, entering our chaos to make it holy.

Peace was born that night in Bethlehem. Peace walked among fishermen and sinners, speaking stillness into storms and forgiveness into shame. Peace touched the unclean, lifted the fallen, and wept beside the brokenhearted. Peace stretched out His arms on a cross and silenced the hostility between God and humanity forever. And Peace still reigns today—stronger than fear, deeper than sorrow, and nearer than our next anxious thought.

Reflections on Peace

The world still wages wars, and our hearts still fight unseen battles—of loss, longing, and uncertainty—but Jesus is still our peace. He steps into our chaos, warms us when the chill of dread settles in, and whispers calm where panic once lived. His presence doesn't promise an easy path, but it guarantees we never walk it alone.

Maybe your battlefield isn't in the desert—it's in your mind, your home, or your heart. Maybe the noise around you feels deafening. But even there, the Prince of Peace is present. He covers you with comfort you can't explain, guards what feels fragile, and reminds you that peace isn't dependent on circumstances—it's found in relationship with Him.

This Advent, as the world rushes and worries, may His peace settle over you like that holy night in Bethlehem. Because peace isn't just coming. Peace has already come.

Peace was born in a Bethlehem barn. Peace slept in a manger. And Peace walks with you today. His name is Jesus.

Prayer

Prince of Peace, thank You for Your steady presence when the world feels uncertain. I surrender my fears and plans into Your hands, trusting that You are working in what I can't control. Quiet my racing thoughts, fill me with Your calm, and anchor my hope in You alone. May Your peace guard my heart today and always. Amen.

The Peace of Joseph's Quiet Surrender

By Lisa Ann Gonzalez

There is a kind of heartbreak that does not make headlines—the kind that arrives before sunrise and rearranges everything you thought you could hold together. Mine came the morning my youngest turned nine. We had moved halfway across the country—away from family, best friends, and the familiar warm embrace of home. I wanted his ninth birthday to prove the sacrifice was worth it. One perfect day, I told myself, and maybe the ache would loosen its grip.

Then, in the dark of the night, the phone rang. My best friend was dying. No flights. No bedside goodbye. His birthday and her last day would now be one in the same. How do you hold a cake in one hand and a breaking heart of grief in the other? How do you sing "Happy Birthday" while mourning a goodbye you cannot speak?

I did not know. With internal turmoil, I stood in the kitchen and wept. I thought of Joseph when he was to take Mary's hand in marriage. He was a steady man with a steady plan—work, marriage, a quiet life. Then came the news: Mary was pregnant, and the child was not his. Joseph had every legal right to clear his name! Instead, he chose mercy. He resolved to dismiss her quietly so as not to disgrace her. Then God asked him to go even further—marry her, raise this Child—Joseph obeyed. Not because it made sense, but because God promised Presence: Immanuel—God with us.

That promise met me in the kitchen with my shredded pieces. I could not give my son a flawless day. I could not rewrite the flight schedules or stop the clock. But I could surrender my right to fall apart and choose love anyway. So, I baked the cake with trembling hands. I wrapped the gifts through tears. I set the table, when we sang, my voice cracked—but every word was true: You matter. Love shows up.

Nothing about the circumstances changed. My friend still gained her wings. The distance stayed. The ache lingered. Yet something quiet settled over the room—a nearness that did not erase sorrow but held it. Peace did not arrive as control; it arrived as companionship. It was not the end of pain but the presence of Jesus in it. Immanuel—God with us.

It is not the absence of heartbreak; it is the open hands of surrender in the middle of it. It is Joseph laying down his right to be correct and discovering mercy's redemptive weight. It is a parent baking a cake with wet eyes and finding Christ is already in the room.

Can you name one "right" you have been gripping—your right to be understood, to be first, to control the ending? Lay it down. Then do one small act of surrendered love: bake the cake anyway, send the text anyway, choose gentleness over vindication. Watch what happens when you stop orchestrating peace and start welcoming His presence. The circumstances may not bow, but your heart will find its steady—held by Immanuel—God with us.

Prayer

Jesus, Prince of Peace, I loosen my grip on how life should be and open my hands and raise them to You. Teach me Joseph's quiet surrender. Meet me where it hurts; hold me where I fear. Help me choose mercy over vindication, obedience over certainty, and love over control. Fill my waiting with Your nearness. Amen.

Unshakable Peace in an Unsteady World

By Elise Daly Parker

While Christmas is the most wonderful time of the year...it can also be the busiest time of the year. The flurry of activities, events, and gatherings meets with the seemingly endless list of to-dos – baking, gift-giving and wrapping, decorating. It's enough to rob us of the peace that Jesus came to bring.

This particular Christmas was no different. Several of my relatives, including cousins, each with at least a baby or two in tow, gathered together. The host's warm, cozy home was bedecked with red velvet ribbons, evergreen boughs, and twinkly lights. Christmas music filled the air. A beautiful, hand-picked Fraser fir was resplendent with colorful bulbs and baubles away from the mayhem in the large porch-turned-playroom across the back of the house, overlooking a pastoral backyard.

Toddlers clamored over chairs, tables, ottomans... with a parent following closely behind to ensure safety.

Babies cooed or cried, depending on the moment. And a few of the kids built wooden block towers only to have them come loudly crashing to the floor. A toy or two acted as a tug-of-war between friends.

Peaceful? No! But it was the stuff of festive, boisterous holiday gatherings with a lively bunch in a tight space. We likely wouldn't come away from this event rested, but we would be full of memories and merriment from a very special day spent among loved ones.

Suddenly, the house went totally dark as the electricity shut off completely. The music stopped, voices faltered mid-sentence, and blackness swallowed the home. In a flash, the Christmas cacophony was silenced. Shortly thereafter, loud wailing and screaming – "Mama," "Daddy" – replaced happy sounds with fearful cries. Though near one another, Moms and dads scurried to reunite with their frightened children. The host clamored for matches and hurriedly lit a few candles on the mantel in the living room, a few more in the kitchen, and still more in the playroom. A soft light now flickered in the otherwise darkened home.

A voice lilted through the chaos, drifting, beckoning to us all from the playroom. We all quietly made our way. There sat my beloved Aunt Patty in her wheelchair, necessitated by the multiple sclerosis that had ravaged her body way too soon. She held a candle, her voice lifted, sweet and strong, but quiet as she sang the heavenly words of Silent Night.

Candlelight shone on the delighted faces of children mesmerized by the holy that hung in the air. One by one, every voice lifted in song. It was a sacred moment in the midst of all the pandemonium. We all took a collective deep breath as peace settled over each one of us. The atmosphere changed completely. We continued singing treasured carols when, just as suddenly, the lights blinked back on.

There was no returning to the festive frenzy. We remained calmer, quieter. There was no loss of cheer, just a reverence for the peace, the holiness, the love, the joy that can be laced throughout this season as we prepare for the wonder of Jesus, the Christ Child, come to us – Emmanuel. As a bit of icing on the cake, soft snowflakes began to flutter right outside the windows of this sacred space, furthering the divine hush that had fallen over our celebration.

We can't force a holy moment like this to stop us in our tracks, to remind us of what this season is truly all about. But we can take a few moments throughout Advent and beyond to turn down the lights, the noise, the chaos of life. Light a candle. Read a passage of Scripture. Play the traditional carols that remind us of the Story of Christmas and prepare our hearts to celebrate the birth of Christ. Amid all the busyness, we can have peace.

Prayer

At this hectic time of year, Lord, we get so bogged down with our To-Do lists. Show me the way to quiet moments during Advent when I am reminded you came to earth to live among us, born to save us! Help me not to miss the sacred moments. Quiet my heart so I can relish the peace you offer even in the midst of noise. Amen!

Unexpected Peace
By Trisha K. Knight

I couldn't believe I was stranded in Germany! Only God can shut the door on my only return flight from England and send me back to Germany. In fact, that's what the border patrol had said. "We have no reason not to let you enter (England), but we will not allow it." The return flight to America was just a couple of days away, but that did not entice the patrolmen. They would not budge.

They will send me back to where I flew in from. I didn't know anyone there, not really. The pastor and his family seemed nice enough. I didn't exactly have a place to stay. I certainly couldn't speak the language; even Germans say it's difficult. I couldn't read the signs to make my way around town. Most of all, I was a very long way from home with nothing familiar to hold onto. I was so lost inside and out about this discord. I could only turn to God. Somehow, through the whole ordeal, I felt the presence of God so tangibly, so intensely. I should have been a mess with all that went wrong that day. I just took each step with overwhelming peace. Times like this, I wish I could feel the arms of God around me, physical arms, but it doesn't work that way.

The original plan was to visit for two weeks, then return to England to help that church get up and running. They had purchased the building a few weeks prior. The carpeting was selected and ordered. Tables and chairs for the cafeteria/kitchenette area were ready. The sanctuary chairs arrived early and were waiting to be placed. There was still a lot to be done for the grand opening.

I felt the presence of God so strongly that day. As they searched through all my items in all my luggage, he was there. When they handcuffed me and escorted me to a locked holding room, he was there. When they took me in a van with bars on all the windows, he was there. I never felt safer and at peace, knowing God was right there with me. That was not the only time this happened. I felt him that day somehow more than any other day. He is with us every day, every hour, and every minute to respond to us. He wants to love every bit of us if we would just allow him space.

One thing I hold to is, you are never alone; God is always within reach, no matter where you may be. From being isolated in a foreign country where you don't speak the language and know no one, to being the only one in a house or apartment that others don't come to visit. Even being out in the open, miles from any other human, with God, you are never, ever alone.

Prayer

Dear Heavenly Father, remain with each individual as they come closer to you while their walk becomes stronger and deeper. Help each one to know your presence and voice more intimately. Settle all uncertainty within and bless them with your abounding peace. Let this peace be where you help them navigate their circumstances. Bless them indeed, with all they need for victory. Amen.

Peace within Your Calling
By Elaine Vallario

As I stepped outside into the damp, cool evening, I admired how the glow of the moon softly illuminated the cloud-covered sky. The air was still as a light rain dusted my coat like newly fallen snow, drops slowly melting into the woolen fabric. In the distance, rugged mountains were softened by a heavy mist, filtering the twinkling lights of mountainside homes, awaiting Christmas morning. This moment, standing in silence, stirred the remembrance of the majestic arrival of the King of kings, born in the most unexpected circumstance, vulnerable to the world as he lay tightly wrapped in the arms of a woman whose heart was full of wonder and praise.

So much uncertainty and possible dangers lay ahead for this young mother as she held her baby close, relying on her faith as her compass. Gripping tightly, in trust, Mary knew the follow-through to her grand calling was divinely woven into her response to the Angel Gabriel when he delivered the news that she would bear God's Son. In one simple sentence in Luke 1:38, she united her will with God's by saying, "'Behold, I am the servant[a] of the Lord; let it be to me according to your word.'"

Notice how the words "let it be" express peace, comingled with fortitude in accepting the task of God's sacred calling on her life. As I stand on the eve of this holy day, there is a comforting weight of awe that rests in my soul as I think of Mary's response to Gabriel. To share in her wonder, I meditate on her words, believing them for myself.

As these words settle in my heart, in quiet resolve, I recognize God's calling set before me within the circumstances of this holiday season. Not knowing the outcomes ahead, I embrace the opportunity to love, show honor, and cherish the moments that I have been given this day and the next as a gift from above. Likewise, I encourage those who are companions of God's grace through good and unexpected times to lift up others in prayer, send messages of hope, and love one another even when it's hard. For we share this charted journey of faith and life, as servants of the Lord, praying the words of Matthew 6:10, "your will be done, on earth as it is in heaven."

May uniting with God's will bring you the peace that surpasses all understanding, and fill your heart with gratitude and praise, for the glory of God, as we stand in the advent of celebrating the greatest gift of all.

For further meditation on the path set before you, read 1 Thessalonians 5:12-18, as we serve the Lord with gladness, wonder, and praise.

Prayer

Heavenly Father, in our struggle to keep a peaceful mind and heart amid busyness and trials, prompt us to discern your will by loving you above all else and following your commands, knowing you are in control, working all things together for good and your glory. In you alone, we find stillness and peace. In Jesus' name, Amen.

The Everyday Arrivals of Jesus

By Holly Burnside

Celebrating Advent as a Church is the celebration of the arrival of Jesus Christ. During Advent, we celebrate both His arrival in Bethlehem as a baby and His arrival to come when He returns for His bride, the Church. In addition, celebrating as an individual amplifies our esteem. Not only should we celebrate together, but we should also celebrate for ourselves all He has done in our own lives.

When I think of the arrival of Jesus, I remember all the moments He has shown up in my life. It didn't just happen once when I gave my heart to him. Rather, it continues to happen each and every day.

Every time I call on the Name of the Lord, He is there. Anytime I enter into prayer or worship, He is with me. In every desperate situation I've found myself in, my savior is the one who saved me once again. Jesus never leaves me hanging. With Him, I am never alone. I never have to feel troubled or afraid. Instead, He is my strength, He is my joy, and He is my everlasting peace.

Readily, my savior stands by with His gentle hands, waiting to catch me when I fall. He never forces His way in, and He never pushes me in the way He wants me to go. Instead, God prepares a path for me and softly illuminates one little step at a time, as He makes sure the things I need will be available at just the right moment.

In perilous times such as these, it fills me with hope to know I never have to worry about a thing. I can live and sleep in peace because I know my Heavenly Father has everything under control. After having a season of life living away from God, to be in right standing with Him now fills me with serenity I cannot fathom. No matter what comes my way or what challenges I face, I remain calm as I immediately turn to my Heavenly Father and my savior, Jesus Christ.

I never need to worry about tomorrow because I know my God is preparing a path of safety for me today. As a Christian, I know the end of the story. It brings me the utmost peace to know; I live on the side of victory. This unbelievable peace I have is available for you too! All you must do is believe in your heart and confess with your mouth that Jesus is Lord.

Every day, I am filled with shalom shalom, which is God's perfect peace. I am hopeful for the arrival of the coming King, as I recognize how He arrives in my life every day prior. He is always faithful, and He arrives with the greatest love we could ever know.

The greatest peace that exists will never be found in the world. But it is certainly within the reach of every single person who calls on the name of Jesus Christ. I encourage every reader to seek the peace I have found in Jesus. I couldn't imagine living another day of my life without it!

Prayer

Jehovah Shalom,

Thank you for filling me with your shalom shalom, your perfect peace! I am grateful I don't have to worry about anything, as you prepare the way and provide the provisions I need to fulfill your will. Help me recognize the places you are arriving in my life. Thank you for the peace which surpasses my understanding! Amen.

Holy Hardship: A Portal to Peace

By Brooke Turbyfill

It was a crisp fall morning when my soft, gray quilt tempted me to stay in bed. But I came downstairs to make breakfast for my daughter, already cuddled up under our homemade finger-knitted blanket, looking at her phone.

I said good morning, and she lamented, "I dooo not want toooo gooo to schooool." We'd recently moved, and the shift had been hardest on her.

She was in a season of waiting—waiting for friendships to deepen at her new school, waiting to embrace the smaller town, and waiting to find activities she loved as much as the ones in our old neighborhood.

It can be tougher to watch our loved ones wait for a breakthrough than to wait for our own. You want to help but don't know how, or worse, you know the hardship is not something you can relieve. They have to go through it.

In my daughter's situation, I knew how much she longed to simply go back to the way things were: private school, familiar friendships, and former team. She wanted to control the circumstance, and not going to the new school that morning seemed like an ideal, albeit temporary, way to do it.

Her desire to go back to bed and return to our hometown is what so many of us do when our circumstances are challenging or involve some waiting. We'd rather revert to what we once knew—even if we recognize it isn't God's plan right now—than embrace a lack of control in our present reality.

How do we find God's peace in the midst of a season we can't control, rush through, or go around? Holy hardship isn't a cute name for something we muster up the strength to endure; in fact, it's the opposite. Our way through the challenge isn't about becoming stronger, but about admitting our need. It involves letting go, a soft relinquishment of our circumstances.

But instead of just letting go, like letting a glass fall to the floor to break, we're invited to let go into something—or, more aptly, let go into Someone. During times of uncertainty, even suffering, it helps to remember the expectation of Advent.

Isaiah 9:6 reminds us that our expectation, where we let our desires and dreams go in waiting seasons, is a Who, a wonderful, full-of-peace Savior:

Reflections on Peace

"For to us a child is born,
    to us a son is given;
and the government shall be upon his shoulder,
    and his name shall be called
Wonderful Counselor, Mighty God,
    Everlasting Father, Prince of Peace."

While you're waiting, expecting your Prince of Peace to show you how He's at work, trust Him not just for your circumstances, but also for your transformation. Using an analogy like 'WAIT' is a memorable way to practice this mindset.

(W) Walk and watch is a phrase that combines a physical walk with listening to God, observing beauty in nature, and watching for the evidence of God's goodness. As you walk, what observations remind you of God's character?

(A) Advocate for your needs, which might mean you take an extra nap or spend time reading. Maybe you listen to music or set aside time each week to have lunch with a friend. What do you need while you are waiting?

(I) Invite God into how you are feeling, holding nothing back. Your Prince of Peace knows it anyway, so include Him as you would a friend. Speaking of friends, invite others into where you are. This isn't the time to pretend that everything is okay. Who can you confide in, someone who will be an encouragement to you on this leg of your journey?

(T) Take heart and trust what Scripture says about you and your belovedness in Christ, and trust His Word that never returns void. (Isaiah 55:11) What does God want to show you about Himself during this season?

Prayer

Prince of Peace, Mighty God, Everlasting Father, Wonderful Counselor, help me to see You as I wait. Give me the courage to let go of what I want to control and trust You to fill me with peace as I do. Amen.

The Pursuit of Unwavering Peace
By Brooke Turbyfill

Our family started a tradition when the kids were little. Getting them to sit still was a challenge, so we kept it short: share one high and one low of your day at dinner. Sometimes, all we could get through were the highs; other times, we ensured each person shared both a high and a low. Our goal was to connect as a family, but our larger goal was to model that it's okay to notice and name the hard stuff. Ultimately, we hope this practice of paying attention sticks with each one of us, no matter where our paths lead.

One thing we didn't count on when we started sharing our highs and lows was that God would teach us a profound truth that's even bigger than naming the difficulties alongside the good. He taught us something about Himself: He is the Ultimate Pursuer, and His peaceful presence can be pursued.

Our simple dinnertime tradition helped us collect our kids' childhood stories: a shiny quarter they found in the driveway, a painful fall from the bike they were learning to ride, a snub from the classmate in the cafeteria, but also a smile from the senior who knew their older sibling. Our kids saw us proclaim God's mercies, too, amidst job loss, illness, and financial struggles.

Collecting stories of God's faithfulness in the midst of difficulty is an unending pursuit of peace. In fact, Psalm 34:14 doesn't just say we should or can pursue peace. It's a command: "Turn away from evil and do good; seek peace and pursue it."

In 1 Kings 18:1, we read about Elijah's word from the Lord: "Go, show yourself to Ahab, and I will send rain upon the earth." As the chapter continues, we learn that Elijah is experiencing one of life's highs. He obeyed God and saw tremendous results—rain, and he got to be involved in God's revelation of His true power, defeating the prophets of Baal. (Read the entire story in 1 Kings 18:1-46). But shortly after that, Elijah is portrayed as fearful, running away, and even despairing of life. (1 Kings 19:1-4)

Isn't this how life feels sometimes? We're experiencing life's best one minute and extreme discouragement the next. How do we walk through life's low moments and still see God's goodness in them?

Our pathway to lasting peace is so simple that we sometimes forget how to access it. The path forward is to pursue God's presence—knowing Him in a deeper, more intimate way—in the midst of life's highs and lows.

The Advent season can bring up feelings of loss, loneliness, or disappointment. It can feel like everyone around us is full of Christmas Smiles Energy while we're left sitting on the sidelines, sad, angry, and maybe even bitter about our lot.

Instead of trying to hide away until the new year comes, try to reflect on how you're feeling, share it with someone else and with God, and then look for something good that coexists with what feels so hard right now. You can use the borrowed prayer included here and make it your own, remembering that you are not alone.

God pursues you just as the angel pursued Elijah at his worst. He gives you permission to feel how you feel and be right where you are. The angel said, "Arise and eat, for the journey is too great for you" (1 Kings 19:7).

Once you've shared your lows with God and recognized what's challenging, ask Him to give you a specific word of encouragement, a job to do that encourages someone else, or a simple task that will help you see His goodness. Just as God made Himself known to Elijah and then equipped him for his calling, God will meet you where you are, show Himself to you, and give you what you need to experience His unwavering peace.

Prayer

Borrowed Prayer: Father God, Jesus, and Holy Spirit, You are here. I recognize it even if I don't feel it. This (name your circumstance) feels really (name your emotion). I am struggling to see what is good right now. Please, help me pay attention to one good thing I can thank You for today. Amen.

Finding Peace in a Season of Waiting

By Kelly M. Sicard

Advent, the four weeks preceding Christmas, marks the beginning of a spiritual season of peace across the globe as we prepare for and await the birth of Jesus. What is the reason for our peace?

We know what came to pass: the Son of God, born in a manger, lived among us, as us, and humbled himself to die on a cross. On the third day, he rose from the dead and opened heaven. Soon after, He appeared to the disciples and sent the Holy Spirit to guide our days on earth. No one but God could've authored this magnificent story, and knowing how it ends brings us peace.

But, just like our lives today, woven throughout this story were periods of waiting and confusion among those who followed Jesus. Mary, Joseph, and the disciples didn't know the details. Only Jesus did.

God doesn't present our life plan with bullet points and slides. He reveals an answer today, another tomorrow, and another five years from now. His direction is gradual, a gentle unfolding that requires us to lean into patient trust.

Peace and patience are closely related. Peace is defined as harmony, freedom from conflict, or a state of wholeness. When we have full trust in God's timeline, fear and resistance fall, and peace rises.

The second chapter of Luke offers insight into the connection between peace and patience as we read what occurs a week after Jesus' birth. Enter Simeon, a Godly man whom the Holy Spirit promised would remain alive until he saw the Messiah, and Anna, an 84-year-old widow-prophet. Simeon and Anna waited many years for a Savior to be born.

When it came time for Mary and Joseph to travel to Jerusalem and present Jesus in the Temple, as required by the Law of Moses, Simeon and Anna saw Jesus. They immediately knew what most did not—that he was the Savior. Simeon declared that he could now "go in peace," and Anna gave thanks and spoke to others of Jesus.

How did Simeon and Anna recognize that this baby was the Son of God? What did they do during those years of waiting to prepare for this remarkable moment? The scripture says that Simeon was led by the Holy Spirit and that Anna fasted, prayed, and never left the

Temple. Their open hearts and disciplined patience gave them clarity to see Jesus for who he really was.

So, what can we do today in our season of waiting? And how do we hold onto peace when the timeline and answers are unclear? We can do what was done in the days of old—fast and pray. We can also serve others and lean into our daily tasks. Waiting on God, when done intentionally, takes strength and courage, and we will grow weary at times. Adding a beautiful ritual to our prayer, like lighting candles, just as we do during Advent, or walking in nature, can anchor us and balance the uncertainty with light.

Prayer

Prince of Peace,

Transform our ordinary time of waiting into a holy season. When we grow weary, draw us nearer to beauty and light to soften our days, and remind us of the promises you've already fulfilled. We trust that in the waiting, we become more like you, which opens us up to clarity and peace. Amen.

Peace in Places Fear Once Lived
By Graye Parsons

It's unattainable, unimaginable, the great mystery of man: peace. How do you find it? How do you create it? What person, place, or thing can fill the hole where peace should abide? You can't. You won't.

When God seems to step back in times of strife, what do we do? I panic. I wonder what transgression deserves His silence. But the truth is: God does not punish with silence. He does not forsake us. He speaks profound wisdom in the quiet, if only we are willing to listen.

Thirteen years ago, I fell for a handsome Marine. His bold presence and stoic face had me dreaming of babies running behind a white picket fence. All I ever wanted was to be a mom.

Soon after we married, deployment orders to Afghanistan halted our plans. He spent nine months overseas serving his country. I spent nine months in agony awaiting his return, while also losing contact with my biological mother. The pain reopened old wounds. My heart stayed heavy, longing for my safe place to return, yet unsure how to carry the weight of absence and fear. Finally, he came home. My heart, though elated, still carried persistent pain. Surely a baby would bring relief.

I became pregnant, but before I could rejoice, I lost the baby. Five more traumatic pregnancy losses followed. Ten years later, my doctor discovered a genetic mutation requiring treatment during pregnancy: One daily shot, and I could sustain a pregnancy. I became pregnant again with my sixth baby, but fear stayed with me. Standing alone one night in my kitchen, tears streaming, I cried, "God, why can't I be calm? Why can't I trust You?"

The answer came swiftly: because I didn't fully believe Him. I wasn't living in total belief of Christ's covering—including over my children. I realized my faith was incomplete in this area; I was clinging to fear rather than fully surrendering to the One who holds all things.

If I believe my soul can be saved, do I also believe our eternal God watches over my children? Yes. I have hope in heaven. I will see my babies one day. This gives me a peace that surpasses understanding, a quiet assurance that God's promises are real. It frees my heart from worry, allowing me to rest in His hands rather than in my own control.

Advent teaches us that God's greatest gifts come through waiting, through darkness, through wombs that seem empty. Mary's yes to the impossible became salvation for the world. My small surrender, trusting God with my womb, became my salvation from fear. The devil doesn't win. What he came to steal, kill, and destroy in my womb belongs to the Creator of the universe. "For all the promises of God find their yes in Him" (2 Corinthians 1:20). There is no better news.

God gave me peace that surpasses all understanding. I could finally enjoy my pregnancy and celebrate the miracle of life. God didn't take my children. He used my suffering to draw me closer to Him.

Christmas didn't come because the world was ready. It came because the world was desperate. My miracle daughter arrived not when I was strong, but when I was finally broken enough to receive her. With my eyes on heaven, I rest easy knowing what the future holds.

"But seek first the kingdom of God and His righteousness, and all these things will be added to you. Therefore, do not be anxious about tomorrow..." (Matthew 6:33-34). Peace isn't found—it's given. And the Giver never changes.

Prayer

My prayer for you, dear reader, is this... Jesus, I am asking on behalf of this reader that you give them supernatural peace, as You have given me. Fill their heart with the Holy Spirit. May they never doubt Your omniscience, and seek You first. Thank You, Lord, for always hearing us. In Jesus's name, amen.

The Timely and Timeless Prince of Peace

By Irene Prabhu Das

This year, 2025, is rapidly moving towards a close. The invitation to peace feels both timely and tender this year. As the year began, I anticipated one workplace shift. However, I was not prepared for the mounting tension and additional unsettling changes that would unfold over the rest of this year. Moreover, actions and decisions resulted in significant and abrupt waves of loss from our workforce. Consequently, uncertainty, worry, and sometimes fear and frustration have framed the tumultuous patchwork of 2025.

About 700 years before the birth of Jesus, the people of Judah were facing a similar situation of personal and national unrest and turmoil. While their context may have been different, they experienced similar feelings and thoughts of uncertainty, fear, and worry due to an impending war with a powerful enemy, Assyria. It was during this time of crisis that God spoke into their lived experience through his mouthpiece, Isaiah. He prophesied an unusual message of hope – a child born for them who had titles reflecting power and authority along with military and protector status, one of which is "Prince of Peace" ("Sar Shalom").

This prophecy of the Prince of Peace was a timely word for the people of Judah. Prophecy, by definition, refers to a future state and a certain time for fulfillment. In this case, 700 years later, the promised babe, Jesus, was born. Why is knowing about the promise of Peace a timely word? The message Isaiah delivered reveals two comforting aspects of our God: 1) He is faithful, and 2) His timing is right. First, God is faithful in hearing us, giving us His word when we need it, bringing to mind what we need to remember, and being present with us in our emotional upheavals. Secondly, Habakkuk 2:3 reminds us there is an appointed time for the fulfillment of God's plan. We trust Him and wait expectantly. He will act on our behalf. Israel had experienced God's miraculous deliverance, victory, and provision throughout their history.

The Prince of Peace is also timeless. His rule of peace is eternal, extending throughout generations. Jesus established the rule of peace when He was born and lived as a human, crucified and resurrected. Through His death and resurrection, He restored the broken relationship between humanity and God, reconciling us to the Father. This peace was made available to anyone who entrusts their lives to Jesus. He alone can forgive.

He alone can heal. Jesus came to give us His peace, unlike the world's peace. His peace is not the absence of conflict, pain, fear, and uncertainty. His very presence of rulership and authority in our lives is our peace. Our peace is not an emotion; instead, He Himself is our peace, shalom ~ peace that is whole and complete, safe and secure.

This Advent season, let us wait expectantly to experience His faithfulness and await His appointed time to fulfill His purpose through our turmoil and uncertainty. Ask Jesus to rule our lives with His timely and timeless peace, as we actively release anxious thoughts, fear of the unknown, unforgiveness, and selfish desires. We can rest in this timely word from Isaiah 26:3: "You keep him in perfect peace whose mind is stayed on you, because he trusts in you."

This year, I have learned that peace is not the absence of chaos; rather, it is resting in His presence as I navigate it. I am learning to surrender to Jesus, who holds all things together. Let this year be your year with the Prince of Peace.

Prayer

Conclude your devotion with a short prayer that flows naturally from what you've shared. It can be a prayer of thanksgiving, surrender, trust, or hope. Prince of Peace, I want very much for you to reign in every area of my life, even in the hurts and uncertainty. Teach me to reflect your peace. As I go through this season, remind me to reach for your timely word in Scripture, help me to know you are near and your peace is real. Amen.

Peace by Piece
By Allison G. Henley

My 16-year-old daughter rehearses for exhaustive hours each week with her high school marching band. Many sunrises and sunsets bear witness to her group's pursuit of excellence. One evening, I sat observing a marching rehearsal in the warm fall weather, and one trombone brashly blared, standing out as much louder than the rest of the group. I was reminded of how a multitude of individual experiences, each with its own volume of impact, make up our lives.

Imagine each instrument as a life experience. Some instruments might blast at a forte, while others might whisper at a pianissimo. Within the dynamics of music, if any one instrument plays too loudly, relative to the whole, it throws the balance off. Alternatively, if any one instrument plays too softly, relative to the whole, it throws the balance off. In our lives, if any one instance of trauma is too loud, or love too quiet, it throws the peace off.

As John 14:27 indicates, Jesus says that He does not give to us as the world gives. Perhaps, as we seek to integrate our worldly highs and lows into the story of our lives, the Prince of Peace offers the precise calibration necessary to soften the peaks and valleys.

What if this concept of peace looks and sounds different than we expect? Might we miss it? What if, instead of embodying one perfectly balanced, grand moment, peace comes in tiny motifs that heal and build up? What if peace looks like integration and harmony? One moment at a time.

God can refine the music of our lives by healing and bringing new life to individual experiences. Taking care to turn the volume down on the blaring pain. Seeking out the life-giving melodies of love and placing a microphone on them. Little by little. Moment by moment. Piece by piece.

What if He lovingly sees each of us in our unique pain and offers the precise volume of healing to offset each trauma? Attention to offset the neglect. Delight to offset the shame. Hope to offset the despair. Each with measured precision. Piece by piece. Peace by piece.

As we enter this Advent season, let's consider which notes of our lives need the balancing touch of our Prince of Peace? Which areas need quieting? Which needs to be highlighted? Where can the existing sounds make slight adjustments into purer harmony? How might we wait in humble expectation of a new sound of peace?

Prayer

Father God, give us ears to hear the harmonies of our lives, which have been calibrated by your peace, and give you all the glory, as we wait expectantly to celebrate the birth of your son, our Prince of Peace.

Finding Peace in Times of Waiting

By Angie Vallejo

After weeks of waiting, the phone call finally came. My husband had interviewed for a long-desired police chief position, and we were certain this was the answer to our heartfelt prayers. We had envisioned a new church, neighborhood, and fresh opportunities. But—the response was no.

It wasn't the first rejection. Throughout his job search, we encountered challenges, setbacks, and the heartbreaking loss of his parents. We prayed and trusted, but the doors stayed shut. Waiting became a part of our daily lives, and we struggled to hold onto hope. At times, it was easy to wonder if God had forgotten us, or if we had misunderstood His leading.

Waiting is never easy. Israel spent centuries longing for their Messiah. Four hundred years of silence stretched between the Old and New Testaments—no prophets, no visions, no new promises. Yet, Advent reminds us that

God's timing is always perfect. He sent Jesus exactly when the time was right (Galatians 4:4).

Like Advent, our seasons of waiting teach us to lean into God's faithfulness. Even when we don't see progress, He is always working behind the scenes. The waiting isn't wasted—it shapes us, strengthens our trust, and brings us closer to Him.

During this season, as we light candles and sing songs of hope, peace, and joy, we are reminded that God drew near to us through Jesus. And we can be assured He will faithfully complete the good work He begins in us (Philippians 1:6). Our waiting may be uncomfortable, but it is never without purpose—and it is always held in the hands of a faithful God.

Prayer

Dear Lord, waiting can be so hard, and at times, I feel forgotten. Yet Your Word reminds me of Your unwavering faithfulness. In this Advent season, help me let go of my worries, trust in Your perfect timing, and find rest in Your promises. Fill me with hope, peace, and joy as I wait in Your presence. Amen.

Reflections on Joy

Abiding Joy in Christ
By Dr. Brittany Javier

What is joy, really? Joy is deeper and greater than happiness. Joy is a deep, abiding gladness of the heart that comes from the Lord, while happiness is a mere fleeting feeling embraced by a culture that has forgotten what true joy is. When we chase happiness through any means apart from Christ, we are not chasing God. When we chase accolades, money, or anything else you may personally place on this list, then we are not chasing God. It's quite simple, really. You can only devote yourself to chasing one God. Are you chasing the God of hope, joy, and peace, or are you chasing the God of happiness?

I have fallen prey to chasing the God of happiness before, and it left me empty and broken. When I chased success or relationships, I always fell short of where I thought I would be. Have I been successful? Well, yes. Have I been in great relationships? Also yes. But, I have also felt the brokenness of putting all my confidence and hope in people and achievements, only to be let down because they were never meant to carry my worship.

When you give a God role to anything or anyone other than God, you will always be disappointed.

Christmas can be a wonderful time of year to slow down in your time with the Lord and rest in Christ and what He has done for us through His birth. I am amazed to think of all that Jesus gave up to come and live a life as a finite human. How could my all-powerful God choose to give Himself a life as a human, knowing that I – and so many others – would still choose to pursue fleeting happiness instead of Him at times? How could He desire us so greatly still?

He can because in His infinite love and kindness, He knows that He is better than the earthly things we chase and that we need Him desperately, even when we don't realize it. He knows that just as Romans 15:13 says, He is "the God of Hope", and we have no true hope apart from Him. He knows that we need Him to fill us with joy because nothing on earth– not even the wonder and excitement of the Christmas season– could ever fill us with true joy. He knows that apart from Him, we will always lack true joy.

This Christmas season, I encourage you to take time to truly sit in the wonder that is Christmas. Take time to truly sit in the amazement that Christ chose to assume a limited human body in order to give us true joy, peace, and hope. As you let these truths from Romans wash over you, allow yourself to look for Jesus in the little moments of the holiday season. Where is He bringing you joy? What is He doing in your life that far surpasses the temporary happiness that we so often chase?

For those of you in a particularly hard season, I encourage you to cling fast to God. Even if your circumstances are fraught with difficulty, God can still be your deep abiding joy purely because He is with you in the hard. Although the holiday season may look different year to year, we can choose each year to look to our kind and gracious Father to fill us with all joy as we reflect on the kindness of Jesus this season.

Merry Christmas, my dear brothers and sisters in Christ. May we always look to Jesus, the great Giver of joy.

Prayer

Father,

I thank you for the season of Advent and for the incredible gift You have given us by sending Your Son. May we keep our eyes fixed on You and our hearts rooted in the joy of Christ this Christmas season. All my love, Amen.

Joy that Remembers
By Laura Lee Pettit

During Advent, when joy is expected to fill every room, grief often slips in quietly, wearing slippers. Yes, it was just a pair of slippers that undid me.

One Sunday morning, while waiting in the church lobby, I noticed an older man walk in – alone, unhurried, calm, and steady. Moving with a familiar shuffle, he was on a mission for his morning cup. We exchanged smiles. Then I saw them – his slippers – and suddenly, my breath caught in my chest.

Tears filled my eyes before I could stop them. That shuffle, those slippers, that quiet determination – it was my father. Or rather, it reminded me of the man he used to be before Alzheimer's began to steal him from us.

My dad had once been full of life and laughter, always ready with a warm greeting, a Scripture, or a joke. He loved his church, loved people, and had a helpful spirit. In his retirement years, he seemed to live to encourage others, often gifting handmade wooden table signs that simply said "Jesus" – to friends, neighbors, even strangers he met.

Alzheimer's changed that. Slowly, painfully, the disease dimmed his light. Memory by memory, we lost pieces of the man we loved. And yet—he never forgot Jesus. During one rare, clear moment, my brothers heard him say, "Jesus is my Savior. What else do you need to know?"

That truth anchored us. His mind was fading, but the joy of salvation was untouched.

That Sunday, grief showed up quietly, wearing slippers. But with it came something unexpected: gratitude. Because joy doesn't always come with laughter or music. Sometimes, it comes with tears and memories - the kind of joy that remembers what mattered most.

We often think joy means being happy, especially at Christmastime. But Advent reminds us that joy and sorrow can hold hands. Real joy comes from knowing that even as we grieve, we are held by a God who came near. Jesus didn't come to erase our pain – He came to redeem it.

Now, I try not to dwell on the painful ending of my father's story. I choose to remember the smiles, the laughter, the joy, how he carried out his life in small everyday gestures, and his deep love for Jesus. I remember the grace that covered his flaws and the God who carried him through it all.

Maybe you're carrying your own quiet grief this season – someone you miss, a loss that still stirs your heart unexpectedly. Let those moments come. Let them soften you, not harden you. Joy can live right there, too – in the memory.

Because when love is real, grief will come. But so will Jesus. And with Him, even our sorrow can turn to joy. Here are some questions to consider: Is there someone you're missing this Christmas? How have you seen God bring joy, even in sorrow? What memory reminds you that love – and joy – still live on?

Prayer

Jesus, You are the good news of great joy that came for all people. Thank You for joy that runs deeper than sorrow, thank You for joy that lingers, even in loss. God of hope, fill us with all joy and peace. Emmanuel, help us hold both sorrow and hope this season, and find You faithfully present in them all.

Real Joy Is Deeper Than Happiness

By Laura Lee Pettit

The world sells us a glittery version of joy each December. Commercials tell us to buy more, give more, smile more. Holiday movies assure us that a happy ending is always just one magical moment away.

But real life—your life and mine—isn't always wrapped in tidy bows and festive endings. It holds sorrow, disappointment, grief, and seasons when joy feels buried beneath layers of pain.

It's been several years since my mom passed, but her presence still visits me in December—especially when I remember our Christmas shopping tradition. When I was in middle school, Mom and I began setting aside a full day during the holidays to shop together—just the two of us.

She didn't drive, so Dad would drop us off at the mall when it opened and pick us up at closing. We were on a mission: secret keepers, gift finders, and treasure hiders. We'd search for the perfect presents, whisper about our surprises, and end the day exhausted and excited. It wasn't fancy—but it was sacred. Even after my daughter—Mom's first grandchild—was born, we continued the tradition, adding baby gifts to all the joy.

Now, the tradition lives on. My daughter and I have set aside our own special shopping day each year. This time, we shop for "the boys"—my husband (her dad), her husband (our son-in-love), and son (our grandson). The legacy of love continues – wrapped up in laughter, shared coffee, and the quiet knowledge that some things are too beautiful to end.

We carry on the joy that was passed down to us. Just like I did with my mom, and my mom did for me. It's not just about the shopping. It's the connection. It's remembering who came before us. It's celebrating what lasts when people are no longer here to join the table or carry the bags.

God wove joy through three generations.

This is the kind of joy Advent invites us into—not the shallow happiness the world offers, but a joy rooted in love, memory, and God's unshakable presence.

Joy isn't always loud. Sometimes it comes quietly—in the form of a tradition, a whispered memory, or a small act that carries the weight of legacy. True joy isn't about escaping pain but finding God's presence in it.

Because in His presence, there is fullness of joy—even when our hearts ache. Here are some questions to consider: What tradition or memory brings you quiet joy during the holidays? How has God met you in moments of both sorrow and celebration? In what ways can you pass joy to the next generation?

Prayer

Lord, thank You for the gift of tradition, togetherness, and the simple joy that flows through love shared across generations. Jesus, in Your presence, there is fullness of joy. Help us hold space for both sorrow and joy this season; to recognize Your presence in the quiet, ordinary moments and notice the joy You are writing into our stories.

A Random Act of Kindness Advent

By Deb Schroeder

Years ago, one evening in early November, my husband and three children were all snug in their beds as I sat up late thinking about the holidays and all that was coming. Truthfully, I was already overwhelmed with the growing to-do list and the expectations I was placing upon myself. Sitting there in the quiet, I soon realized my heart was growing heavy with weariness rather than growing excited with anticipation of the Advent season.

I remember as a child, I loved everything about the Advent Season because I knew it meant hope, anticipation, and joy. Every Advent, I witnessed my childhood church transformed with a large Advent wreath made of greenery, ribbons, and candles hanging from the ceiling. I loved walking in and seeing a new candle lit each Sunday. For me, that wreath wasn't a countdown until Christmas and presents; it was a promise of a coming celebration of Jesus.

Letting out a deep sigh, I realized I longed for this Advent season to be more than gifts, decorations, and all the holiday stress. I wanted our days and nights to be intentional in terms of experiencing true joy. And, I wanted my children to experience joy that lasted far beyond the holidays.

It was in those still, uninterrupted moments that I heard the whisper from God to teach my children about the joy that comes from serving. I wanted my children to understand the beauty and humbleness in Philippians 2:3-5. I wanted them to recognize the value in others and understand their needs.

The following week, I spent time creating my own version of an Advent calendar for my family. I couldn't wait for December 1st to arrive because we would begin our 24 Random Acts of Service as a way to be the hands and feet of Jesus during the holiday season. Rather than a simple countdown for Christmas, our focus would be on praying for others and loving them. We would prepare our hearts to celebrate the birth of Jesus by loving like Jesus did.

Each day, we selected a way to serve, and each day, we became more excited for this moment. We held doors open for people at the mall; we pushed shopping carts back at the grocery store one evening. We bought a man a new meal after he accidentally spilled his drink on his tray at the food court. We baked and delivered cookies for the fire department and police station. We made some meals for families in need. We shopped and delivered gifts for local children in crisis. We made cards for residents in a nursing home.

And, with each random act of kindness, I could see the joy filling my children's hearts. They couldn't wait for the next moment to serve someone, and to my heart's content, we were seeing how service and joy meld together beautifully.

Twenty-four random acts of kindness brought the love of Jesus to the forefront of our holidays, and it allowed us as a family to both give and experience pure joy. Each act of service was like unwrapping a gift from under the tree, not knowing what was inside and not expecting how much you would love it. We spread joy to those we surprised by simple acts of kindness. We moved quickly and humbly, pointing all praise back to Jesus. After all, it wasn't about us; it was about serving others.

Twenty-four random acts of kindness painted the joy and anticipation of Christmas beautifully across our hearts. It captured what the joy of Christmas is really about – serving and loving others.

Prayer

Heavenly Father, prepare my heart for the joy that awaits this Advent Season. Help me to see the opportunities to be the hands and feet of Jesus and guide my heart to action so that I may love others well. I pray that the joy of serving others stays with me well beyond Advent. In your name I pray. Amen.

Elisha Discovers Advent
By Sandra Yaude

Elisha looked out the front window. He saw his neighbor, Mr. Doberstein, heading toward the woods, his axe slung over his shoulder. Elisha quickly grabbed a jacket and raced out the door.

Mr. Doberstein, or "Mr. D" as Elisha called him, had become like a grandfather to him. Living alone, Mr. D was very grateful for this special relationship.

Catching up with Mr. D, Elisha asked, "Where you headed?"

"I'm going to cut me down some special limbs."

"What's special about tree limbs?" Elisha asked.

"It's what they'll be used for that makes 'em special," Mr. D explained.

Elisha shrugged. He followed Mr. D. as he chopped down a number of large, full evergreen branches, even letting Elisha cut some. Together they carried them back to Mr. D's workshop in his barn.

"Now, how 'bout a cup of hot cider?

"Sure!"

Sitting quietly in Mr. D's kitchen, Elisha asked, "Whatcha gonna do with those limbs?"

"They're for a very special project."

"Oh? What?" Elisha pressed, his curiosity aroused.

"You ever hear of an Advent wreath, Elisha?"

Elisha thought hard. "Don't think so."

"It's a very special tradition our family has enjoyed for generations. Think of it as something to remind us of something else. What big holiday is coming up soon?"

"Christmas!!"

"Exsss-actly. When you weave fresh evergreen branches into a wreath, it becomes an Advent wreath," explained Mr. D.

"What's Advent?"

"You meet me at the barn tomorrow morning and I'll tell you all about it," Mr. D invited.

At 8 am the next day, Elisha walked into the barn to find Mr. D already working with the branches.

"Morning, Elisha."

Elisha got closer to see what he was doing. "Why are you putting the limbs in a circle?"

"A circle is a symbol of eternity, just like God's love is everlasting," explained Mr. D. Elisha agreed that made sense. "We use evergreen branches because they symbolize the everlasting life we can have through Jesus."

Together, they fashioned the limbs into a beautiful wreath. "Now, come over here." Mr. D led Elisha to an old trunk. He lifted the heavy wooden lid and removed a long white box. "Carry this over to the workbench," he instructed.

Placing it down gently, Elisha asked, "What's in here?"

"A very important part of the Advent wreath. Take a look."

Elisha lifted the lid. "Candles?"

Mr. D laughed and took out five candles–three purple, one pink and one white.

"What are they for?"

Pointing to the colored candles, Mr. D explained, "These are lit, one each week before Christmas, to remind us of Jesus' message to the world of hope, faith, joy and peace."

"What about the white one?" asked Elisha.

"Ah, that is the Christ candle, only lit Christmas Eve. It reminds us of Jesus' purity and of His light coming into the world."

They carried everything to the kitchen. Mr. D got out a round candle holder and placed it in the wreath's center. They put the candles in place, then stood back admiring their work.

"Just a minute," said Mr. D, rushing out of the room. He returned with his large family Bible and placed it next to the wreath. "Now we're ready," he said, a satisfied smile gracing his face.

"What's next?" asked Elisha.

"Advent starts Sunday. How about you come over about 6:30? We'll do the Advent devotion time together, and I'll share more about what it means to prepare our hearts to receive Jesus' message of love and salvation."

"Sure. 6:30 sharp!" Elisha beamed with great anticipation.

Sharing Advent devotions became a special tradition for Elisha and Mr. D.

Prayer

Lord, life goes by so fast and so much can be forgotten. Help us slow things down and focus on what is truly important. Encourage us to make time to pass along time-honored traditions to the next generation that help prepare our hearts to receive you this Christmas. Amen

Joy because of Jesus
By Whitney Britton

I hear my preacher say these words as I look up at him, nodding to show understanding and attentiveness. Yet, inside my mind, I can't help but think "Hmm… this verse doesn't feel quite right to me", and I'm instantly reminded of my humanity and my sinful nature.

I can think of a lot of things that bring me joy. A walk outside. A yummy meal. A good book. The sound of my son's laughter. A much-needed date night with my husband. All of those things? They bring me joy. Trials, troubles, and tribulations? I must admit that joy is not quite the first emotion that comes to mind.

Yet, God's word is true, and the Bible has these words in it for a reason. So why did God tell us to consider trials as joy?

James 1:3-4 talks about mature faith. Ahh, now that thought- the thought of mature faith, lacking nothing, well that feels good. That feels joyful. That's what I want. Complete faith. I'm sure that's what you want too, friends.

I'm reminded that joy is not always circumstantial. We live in a fallen world. We are surrounded by sin, and trials are one of the only guarantees in this world. It's why James says "whenever" you face trials, not "if ever".

We can have joy, not knowing what tomorrow will hold, because of Jesus. We can have joy in the midst of these trials because of Jesus. We can have joy when life feels everything but, because of Jesus.

Prayer

Lord, whatever the trial, whatever the circumstance, may my faith be strengthened. May my faith be made complete. May I find joy because of Jesus, who paid the ultimate sacrifice and died on the cross for the remission of our sins.

The Courage to Raise
By Vivianna C Welflin

During the season of Advent, it's so easy, almost necessary, to occupy ourselves with things of the world. It's tempting to spend hours in front of the TV watching Christmas movies and football games.

While we sit and watch, the commercials taunt us. It's not even necessary to leave your recliner anymore. Just point your smartphone at the TV screen and "scan the code". We have lists of things that must be done—shopping, baking, and parties.

This time of the year can be so stressful, and as a result, it's easy to put our spiritual life on the back burner. Recently, a friend reminded me to go outside when things get crazy. "Go look for the flowers," they said.

I was walking through the yard and I noticed how overgrown it had become. Farthest from the main path was a very tall weed. Normally, we would've pulled it at first sight, but it had grown to two feet tall.

I stopped and knelt to take a close look. I noticed the long stalk that had grown from its core. At the tallest point, I saw a crown of buds which had begun to blossom into a beautiful, tiny bouquet of purple flowers. My joy came from the fact that I was led by my Lord to see and contemplate it.

I thought about the possibility of that weed being cut before it had time to blossom. I think of "the cut" being the moments when we deny our Lord. It's like cutting Him off mid-sentence. I considered that I was just like that weed, and my Lord was patiently waiting for me to blossom. He waits for all of us.

I felt special that He would show this to me and that I understood the depth of His message. I know He just wants to spend time with us. I have been blessed to see Him in these natural miracles, and I am overjoyed. Because I slowed my pace and deliberately took the time to just be with my Lord, I was able to see Him in a crown of flowers. Where do you see Him?

Prayer

Lord, as we wait and prepare to celebrate the birth of our Savior, I pray for our world and for the souls who are awaiting their season of blossoming. I pray their longing is satisfied in Your loving embrace. I pray they will experience absolute joy with You. Amen

Joy vs. Happiness
By Dawn Marie Thompson

As God's chosen people once gathered in the days of Nehemiah, they celebrated and listened attentively to the reading of the Law, just as the prophet instructed them. In much the same way, we gather during this Advent season—around our tables, sharing food and drink in celebration—to remember the arrival of our Savior to the earth. Nehemiah also reminded the people to give to those in need, so everyone could share in the festivities and remembrance of the Lord.

Life can be difficult at times. The day-to-day responsibilities and chaos can quietly steal our joy. Through my own journey—both in helping others and walking through personal struggles—I realized my joy had faded. I tried to reclaim it through my children and grandchildren, my church family, and the fulfillment I found in work. However, nothing truly restored it, because as Scriptures teach, "the joy of the Lord is our strength." True joy can only come from Him. During this sometimes-emotional holiday season, we must seek

God Himself—not happiness—so that this fruit of the Holy Spirit may not just return to our lives but flourish.

I've learned that happiness is not the same as joy. We can be happy and still lack what God has for us. You can find fulfillment in family, career, or community, and still not possess the deep, abiding joy that only Jesus Christ can give. Joy is a gift from God—a bubbling, overflowing gladness that cannot be contained. It is the desire to please the One true God, the Maker of the universe, and have your relationship with Him be the focus of your life.

This joy is supernatural. It strengthens us. It is God's way of covering our lives with His safety and protection, just as He did in the time of Nehemiah. His joy brings strength to our weary bodies when life's demands drain us. It brings strength when illness strikes—whether through viruses, chronic pain, or cancer. It strengthens our minds when anxiety or depression tries to rob us of peace. And, it strengthens our hearts and emotions, helping us live balanced and complete lives, even amid pain or loss.

Let His delight in you be your refuge. Let it silence the noise of social media, television, and the harsh words of others. Let it heal emotional wounds and bring balance back to your soul. Let His joy strengthen and sustain you. Let Him quiet the busyness of the Season and bring His true joy unto you.

As we light the pink candle to signify this emotion, let us prepare our hearts to receive joy and receive the Christ anew, as we refocus our lives toward Him.

Prayer

As we gather, let us remember your people during the time of Nehemiah. Help us be strengthened with true joy, achieved from your Holy Spirit. May we accept this joy—not just happiness—may our spirit be filled and bubbling over, so life's demands do not take our joy away, but we can maintain it, even when stressful times arise.

Waiting for Joy
By Lacey Hicks

It's easy to get discouraged, especially in Advent. There can be pressure to have a picture-perfect family and Christmas. This often isn't the case for various reasons. Yet this is also the time that we're reminded that "nothing is impossible for God". It's not on our own strength.

It's hard to wait on God's timing. It's easier to give up - Elizabeth had likely given up on ever having a child - or take matters into our own hands.

In my case, I had trouble getting and keeping a full-time job. I have a learning disability and come off as "awkward." It is hard to admit as my parents had successful careers and my brother currently works for Google. Meanwhile, I went to so many interviews with nothing. But on God's timing, I got a job with a nonprofit that works with people with disabilities. This was right after I was going to move away from an expensive area with no family. I still work for this nonprofit today as a job coach. It's allowed me the opportunity to show

God's love to clients. There can be joy in seeing clients improve at work or just getting to know them better.

I also went through a discouraging time of being single. I was 25 before I dated for more than a few months. I then got married even though we had issues because I didn't want to wait on God's timing. Things got bad enough that we divorced only a few years later. Now I'm remarried in a much healthier situation, because I waited on God's timing. It's a reminder that what's important is the marriage - all the decades that follow the wedding - rather than solely the wedding itself.

God knows what you're waiting for and can do miracles. He wants there to be joy in your life. In fact, one morning at church, a man came up to me and said, "God wants to give you this one-word message: joy." We may not always know the reasons for a season of waiting, and they may not be answered in a way that's expected. But we can be sure that God loves us and wants the best for us. He came into the world so we could be reconciled to Him. He also wants us to have joy where we are right now. It brought me so much joy when I finally became a job coach and then finally met my now husband. It deepened my relationship with God and provided me the ability to meet people I never would have otherwise.

Prayer

Dear Lord, you know what we're waiting and longing for. You want there to be joy in our lives. Please support us in our time of waiting and give us the strength to not lose hope that circumstances will ever improve. We know you want a relationship with us and have reasons for your timing.

The Great Advent Glimmer Hunt

By Janell Rardon

I sat in the backseat of my daughter Brooke's car, right next to my fifth grandchild, six-week-old Baby June. I nestled closely to June, placing my right hand on her little chest and my left hand on the handle of her car seat. I made sure she was safe and secure.

While we were driving to enjoy an afternoon of Christmas Open Houses, Brooke sang along to her favorite Christmas music. I sat in the back with a huge smile on my face, being present to both baby June and her delightful mama. Brooke knew the words to every song. As I watched Brooke, I smiled. "She's always loved Christmas," I said to myself. Her right hand floated up in the air as she worshipped and snapped and danced—never missing a beat. I looked over at baby June, soaking in the joyous atmosphere of this magical afternoon adventure.

Brooke's joy was contagious. That's the beautiful thing about joy: it's contagious. Joy begets joy.

I'm guessing that is what the psalmist meant when he penned these beautiful words in Psalm 16:11: "In Your presence, there is fullness of joy."

Right in the middle of this seemingly ordinary car ride, I experienced what psychologists call a glimmer—a tiny micro-moment of joy that unleashes an immediate sense of inner peace and calm. Glimmers typically occur when you least expect them, often take your breath away, and appear in the most ordinary ways. Their surprising visits can happen at any time, in any place, and in any way, shape, or form. The only requirement is that we must activate our five senses, awaken our hearts, and anticipate their presence all along the path of our day.

Imagine with me right now. If you can, close your eyes. Hold out your hands. Sense that God is placing a divine invitation in them. Now open your eyes. Feel the soft linen envelope. Notice your name, hand-lettered in shimmering, buttery 14-carat gold ink. As you open it, you see it's also lined with shimmering, buttery 14-carat gold paper. This invitation, fit for a Queen, is written to you. Yes, you! When you're ready, read it slowly:

Dear One, I invite you to an Advent season unlike any you've experienced. Will you join me in resisting the craziness of the season's commercialization and chaos and instead activate a pensive, childlike anticipation of glimmering joy? When you wake up every day, I will be waiting. Together, we will go glimmer hunting. We'll sing loudly and giggle with great joy. Let me fill your heart with contagious joy. Watch and see how everyone in your presence shares in your joy. With abundant joy, God.

Prayer

Father, today I accept your invitation to go glimmer hunting. I will begin each morning of this Advent season with heart and hands open to receive the glimmers being sent my way. When I get caught up in the hurry and scurry and worry of a rushing world, I pray that I slow myself down. Right now, I'm picking up my glimmer wand and preparing to sprinkle glimmer dust everywhere I go. Amen.

Finding Joy in Everything
By Joy Caswell

During Advent, the world tells us to find joy in shopping, decorations, and celebrations. The real source of joy came wrapped in swaddling clothes, lying in a manger. Jesus is God's greatest revelation of life. Through him, we see what perfect joy looks like. A joy that suffered on the cross, defeated death, and still invites us into the Father's presence today. When we make time to dwell in His presence through prayer, quiet reflection, or worship, our hearts are filled with that same joy David described. Our distractions fade, and we remember that our joy doesn't come from what we have, but rather who we have.

I remember my first visit to Wyoming, how strongly I felt the presence of God as I stood at the base of the Tetons. The vast size of the mountains right in front of me, the peace and joy that instantly flowed over my body and my mind.

My visit was at the end of fall, after all the tourist attractions had closed for the season. It was the quiet time before the skiing season began. The sound of the river flowing across the rocks behind my cabin, and the majestic scenery everywhere I looked, even the moon felt like it was perfectly placed. I took so many photos during that trip; I was elated with joy. The moose, elk, deer, and buffalo were all out grazing without a single care in the world. It felt like they invited me over for a visit to spend time with them and God. Not only did I have the best seat in the house, but I got the best sleep of my life on that short trip to the mountains. It was so good for my soul, breathing in that crisp mountain air, and feeling so close to God.

The sunsets were amazing that week. It was like God had hand-painted them just for my trip. The colors were so vibrant against the snow-covered peaks. Being out in nature is where I connect best with God. It fills my heart with joy beyond measure and allows me to refuel after all the negativity in this world. It reminds me that even in seasons of hardship, loss, or uncertainty, God's presence remains constant.

This Advent, may Psalm 16:11 draw you back to the presence of Joy. Let his light fill your heart, and may his nearness remind you that true joy isn't under the Christmas tree; it is already within you, because Christ has come. Start a new tradition this Advent, get outside and do something that brings you joy. Whether it is taking a sleigh ride, spending time with family at a local festival, or picking up a new hobby. Leave the devices in airplane mode and enjoy each moment, and then take note of all the joy these memories brought to your heart.

Prayer

Gracious heavenly father,

Thank you for showing me the path of life through Jesus Christ. Help me to rest in your presence and find the fullness of joy there. This Advent season, draw my heart closer to You so that Your joy may overflow in me and bring light to others. Amen

From Abortion's Ashes to Joy in Emmanuel

By Melissa A. Mayer

Advent is a season when the world waits for a baby—the birth of Jesus, the Redeemer. Churches glow with candlelight, voices rise in carols, and hearts anticipate the arrival of hope. But for the woman who has experienced abortion, this season can feel painfully complicated. While others celebrate the coming of a child, you may carry the silent ache of a life (or lives) ended—a baby whose arrival never came.

Abortion is a word we rarely hear in church, especially during Advent. For years, I kept my story hidden, not even admitting to myself that I was grieving. I had no intention of testifying I'd had an abortion – much less confessing I'd made that dreadful trek to the clinic five times. I wore a mask of strength, convinced that if I didn't acknowledge the loss, maybe it would fade away. But the truth is, silence doesn't heal. Sometimes, we don't recognize our grief because we've never been told we have the right to grieve. We keep our secret, not realizing that the reason we hide it is shame or misplaced pride.

Advent's waiting can feel like a cruel contrast. The world waits for a baby, but you may feel like your waiting ended in regret. There's a temptation to believe you're disqualified from joy, that your story is too broken for celebration. Maybe you've tried to convince yourself it wasn't really a baby, just to survive the ache. But deep down, something sacred was lost—and that loss deserves to be named and mourned.

The Bible reminds us of the nearness of the Lord, that His entire plan from Genesis to Revelation is the restoration of our relationship with Him. This is the heart of Advent: Emmanuel—God with us. Not only with those who appear to have it all together with no reason to hide their faces, but with those who mourn, those who grieve, those who feel unworthy. God draws near to us in our deepest pain. He doesn't ask us to hide our grief or pretend our story is pretty. He invites us to take off the mask, to own our story, and to let Him step into the silence.

Joy in Advent isn't about ignoring the past or forcing a smile. It's about discovering that Jesus came for you—right where you are. He came to bind up your broken heart, to lift the weight of shame, and to offer you a joy that rises from the ashes. You are not disqualified. Your grief is real, and your healing matters to God more than you can comprehend.

This Advent, set aside a quiet moment to light a candle—just for you. As you watch the flame, invite Jesus into your grief, your silence, and your story. Write a note to yourself, naming what you've lost and what you hope to find. Let this act be your first step toward unmasking grief and welcoming the joy only Jesus can supply.

As the world waits for a baby, remember: Emmanuel—God with us—means God is with you. He came to break your silence, to heal your heart, and to restore your joy. You have the right to grieve, and you have the right to hope for joy. Let His love unmask your pain and invite you into the joy of being fully known and fully loved.

Prayer

Emmanuel, thank You for being God with us—even in our grief and silence. Help me take off the mask of shame and invite Your healing into my story. Restore my joy, teach me to grieve with hope, and use my journey to bring light, healing, and, yes, JOY, to others this Advent. Amen.

A Branch Rises

By Heather Cruz, M.Ed.

The title "Ugly Christmas Tree" doesn't even begin to capture the significance of our beloved tradition. Every year, our Christmas tree search is a long-awaited adventure. Snow pants swish, swish, swish through the rugged path, and boots fill with cold, pure white chunks of snow as we wander through the woods in search of the perfectly imperfect tree.

This is not just any tree. It is a tradition that holds the same weight in our family as the ugly Christmas sweater party: strange, joyful, full of laughter, and stories. But there are rules. Our tree must meet three criteria:

It must take a long time to find. This is a journey, not a transaction.

It must come with a special story. Something that makes people laugh, pause, or say, "Only your family would pick that tree."

And it must scrape the 14-foot ceiling—at times, we saw the bottom off of a much taller tree with a chainsaw, but we always make room for the 60-year-old family star on top.

One year, our tree looked more like a giant shrub than a pine, with a lone branch sticking out in the middle like a hand waving hello. That tree lives in family lore. We still talk about "the waving tree"—how something so odd, so imperfect, became the centerpiece of our home, our laughter, and our joy. That waving branch did not ruin the tree; it made the tree. It was what it was meant to be. In the same way, that waving branch reminds us of the deeper truth of Christmas. It points us to Jesus, the essence of this season.

In Romans, Paul speaks of a branch growing from Jesse's roots—Jesse, the father of King David. This image echoes back to Isaiah 11, where it reminds us that a shoot will form from the stump of Jesse.

The author of Isaiah reminds us that the shoot, that branch, will bear fruit. It's a powerful image: a tree cut down to a stump—nothing left but what seems dead and forgotten. But from that stump, a Branch rises. A Savior is born.

Jesus is that branch—the one who grew from a simple, broken family line. The one who came not in perfection, but in humility. He brings new life, joy, and hope to a weary, broken world.

Just like our "ugly" tree, Jesus chose not to arrive in a polished or pristine way— He arrived in a humble town, from a humble woman, and in a humble stable.

When guests walk through our door at Christmas, their reactions to our tree say it all. Some gasp. Some laugh. Some struggle to understand our attachment to what looks to them, like a crazy mess. Once the shock wears off, they begin to see what we see.

They realize that this tree means something deeper. Christmas isn't about perfection. It's about presence.

It's about coming as you are—messy, tired, imperfect— and being loved anyway.

The kids who sleep under our tree, the guests who sink back into the couch to listen to Christmas stories year after year—they get it. They sense the peace and joy that radiate from our tradition, our tree, our special branch. Not because it's perfect. But because it's real.

Joy overflows from that tree just as hope overflows from the Branch of Jesse. Because the true meaning of Christmas is this: Jesus came for the imperfect. For the cut-down. For the overlooked.

For you and for me.

Prayer

Lord, Branch of Jesse, we thank you that you bring a promise of hope to all of us. The hope you bring comes from your life, your grace, and your love for each of us. We pray that you will surround us with joy this Advent season.

ReJoy

By Lisa Ann Gonzalez

It is Christmas. The world glitters with manufactured joy while you are drowning in your kitchen at midnight, staring at dishes and a heart that will not stop breaking. Perhaps you are in your car in some parking lot, hands gripping the steering wheel, trying to remember how to breathe. Or you are in that thin, terrifying space between the wrapping paper and the smile you are wearing—where no one sees your smile is as temporary as the bow on gifts; ready to be ripped off.

Most of the world seems to have unlocked some door to joy that you cannot find. The rest of us? We are searching the wreckage of our own hearts for proof that joy—real joy, the kind that knows about pain and chooses to exist anyway—is still possible.

Is it possible that joy is not something you are supposed to manufacture in your chest like some spiritual achievement? Is it possible that joy is something you can receive again? Not "rejoice"—the command wrapped in guilt. Re-Joy. Joy again. A return to what was always there. Behind the senses, like a shadow that never leaves you.

I live by the beach, and the ocean is my refuge. I go to the water's edge where sand meets water, where everything blurs into one, there—in the threshold—I meet God. The ocean is beautiful. It is also dangerous. It can swallow you whole. I stand there anyway, knee-deep, feeling the saltwater, and it reminds me: beauty and danger can exist in the same moment. I can still choose to turn toward the light.

When I was a child, I was terrified. Everything hurt. Everything was too big, too loud, too sharp. But I remember being held. I remember knowing—the way a child knows things before language arrives—I was loved. Loved in a way nothing could strip me of. His arms were there. They made me safe.

I am older now, and I still have moments standing in the mirror, feeling the weight of all my failures, all my not-enoughness. A voice whispers: You are not enough. You will never be enough. Look at what you lack. And I want to fall apart. But then, I remember: I am held. Even now. Especially now.

Psalm 23 reminds me of green pastures, still waters, and of a love that restores my soul. Not someday. Now. In this moment of restoration, I am already whole, already safe, already loved. I am already enough.

Jesus speaks directly to the ones struggling, carrying heavy burdens, the brokenhearted, to me. He tells us to put down our loads. Learning from Him, and we will find rest. (Mat:11:28-29): He is inviting you to receive it. Just as you are.

Your Re-Joy might look like finally sleeping without nightmares. Standing at the checkout line and not crying. A whispered prayer in the dark. Sitting by the ocean, and breathing it in. It still counts.

Now comes the hardest part: learning to forgive yourself and to stop prosecuting yourself for what He has already pardoned. God has already forgiven you— every broken part, every shame, every 3 A.M. moment when you remember all the ways you have failed.

Already forgiven. Rest in His arms. Breathe. Remember. Receive. Where the Father meets the broken, there too, you will find Re-Joy.

Prayer

Father, I am in the dark, meet me where I am. Hold me when I cannot smile. Remind me, I am not alone, not broken beyond repair, not beyond Your reach. Teach me to receive Your Joy and grant me the courage to forgive myself. Let me find ReJoy–not in happiness, but in Your unshakeable love. Come, Lord Jesus. I am here where your love meets my joy. Amen.

Joy in the Now
By Stephanie Judy

We waited a long time for a baby. God sent three who went ahead of us to heaven. Bereft, I closed the door to the idea of grieving another loss. The daughter who had made me a bonus mom many years before was in college. We sold our home and embraced our "empty nester" life stage, but the month we signed a lease on a tiny rental, I learned I was pregnant. I felt surprised and hesitant to celebrate, unsure how long I'd carry this child. But God knew that we would expect him in January and the upcoming months would be the most special Advent season.

On Christmas Eve, I fell asleep warm and happy from our daughter's homecoming, but awoke to painful contractions as the littlest life became the biggest Christmas present. Nothing went according to plan. An arduous labor birthed a painful season that included months of therapy for me to walk again. I battled through a dark year of the soul in which I succumbed to doubts that perhaps this suffering indicated that God didn't love me or had abandoned me. I wavered in my surety of God's goodness through the sleepless days.

Years later, I finally bared my soul to Jesus, asking, "Were you there in the hospital room when everything went wrong? Did you leave me?" The required vulnerability felt like a back-alley open-heart surgery. For the first time, I noticed my cracked-open ribs, a wound long neglected in the wake of trauma. My heart throbbed with a fear of no reply. But, ever faithful, I heard Him reassure me. *I was there. I never left you. I will redeem your pain.* In a moment, My redeemer sewed me back together by treating the wounds that I'd hidden and held onto in isolation. True healing began. He opened my eyes to all of the times He'd tried to speak to me, all of the people He'd placed into our lives to help us, every good and perfect gift from the Father of heavenly lights. Specks of joy I hadn't noticed seemingly flitted onto the scene.

To see such specks of joy requires focused vision. Equestrians utilize "look-up" glasses that limit the eyes from glancing downward. Riders must look straight ahead to achieve clear vision. I wish I had a pair of spiritual "lookup" glasses that kept my eyes from the distraction of trials. But perhaps without noticing in the now, He is fitting us for these. Forming us through the trials, showing us that the longer we fix our eyes on Jesus, the less the distractions take up space, and the clearer He gets. One day, may it be just a pinhole, where all we see is Him.

When I look backwards at our story, I wonder when was the beginning of joy? As I try to trace it, I see the bigger story. Did joy enter when Jesus was resurrected? Or perhaps earlier at Jesus' birth? I see the fullness of joy, started long ago, both for me and for all time. But I almost didn't recognize it until I was on the other side of the trial. I know another trial will come, but this time I want to see the joy from the beginning. Reach out and cling to the hope even when I can't see it yet, even when I only hear distant future echoes reverberating. I want to cling tight to the hope of Jesus until my spirit sings to my soul the story. Until I know full well. Until I see his face.

Prayer

Heavenly Father, You are so good. Thank You for the mysterious blessing of joy in the midst of trial, pain and suffering. Teach me to affix my attention so intently on You that all the distractions of this world fade away. Please open my eyes to see every good and perfect gift from You. In Jesus' name, Amen.

Joy in the Midst of Scarcity

By Shannon Floyd

Tears rolled down my face as I walked down Newbury Street in Boston, a place known for luxury and affluence because of its designer fashion, upscale dining, and high-end apartments. This did not seem like a place for a woman wearing a shirt from a box store, driving a well-worn Hyundai, and carrying a box of free meals. But in that moment, I felt like the richest woman in the world.

Living in one of the most expensive cities in the nation, my salary barely covered the basics. Groceries felt like a luxury. My heart desired the Freshly brand ready-to-eat meals delivered to your door. But my wallet called for ramen noodles.

With only $20 to cover the next two weeks, those meals were not an option, so I quickly clicked off their website. I prayed for provision for food, and then I waited.

About two weeks later, I was assigned, as part of my job, to interview a man who lived in one of those

Newbury Street's upscale apartments. As we met in the lobby, the concierge handed him a delivery box that arrived while he was out. We rode the elevator together and then chatted through the interview.

As I reached for the door to leave, he stopped me. "I forgot to cancel this," he said. He held out the box he received from the concierge. He insisted I take it.

Inside were Freshly meals -$100 worth. This was an answered prayer. Not just provision, but the exact meals I had longed for. My frustration over his absence the week before, when we were originally scheduled to meet, disappeared instantly. That delay was divinely orchestrated.

In the midst of scarcity, God had whispered His presence through provision. And this provision was so precise, beyond coincidence and timely, it bore the unmistakable fingerprint of God.

It reminded me of the widow of Zarephath in 1 Kings 17. She was preparing a final meal for herself and her son before surrendering to starvation. Then Elijah appeared, asking for bread. She obeyed, and God met her with provision of oil and flour. She didn't receive abundance; she received enough. Enough to remind her that she was seen. Enough to whisper, "I am here."

As I walked back down Newbury Street, past the luxury storefronts and shoppers wearing designer jeans, I didn't feel envy. I didn't feel a lack. I felt joy. Not because my circumstances had changed, but because I had been reminded of God's presence and love. Like Hagar in the wilderness, I could say, "You are a God of seeing" (Genesis 16:13). His provision didn't overflow; it was just enough. That box of food didn't erase my bills. It didn't fill my pantry or solve tomorrow. But it was enough to know I was seen.

Joy isn't found just in abundance, but it is also found in scarcity, where our faith is stretched. Scarcity has a way of stripping us down to the essentials. It reveals what and who we truly rely on. And when God meets us there, joy becomes more than a feeling. It becomes a testimony. On a street lined with luxury I couldn't afford, I found something far more valuable. I found joy.

If you find yourself walking through your own version of Newbury Street during this season, surrounded by what you don't have, remember this: joy isn't reserved for times of abundance. It's found in the moment you realize that the God of abundance is also the God of enough. Our joy is rooted in His presence, not our circumstances.

Prayer

Lord, may we always be reminded of Your faithfulness and the beauty of being seen by You. When the world measures worth by wealth, remind us that true riches are found in You. Thank You for delighting in blessing us. Even in scarcity, joy is possible because You are present, and in Your presence, joy overflows. Amen.

Remain in Me

By Crystal Dawn Modlin

A few years ago, after the holiday season had ended, I found myself sitting in my living room with a cup of coffee, feeling empty, exhausted, and lacking joy. We had just finished a busy season loaded to the gills with all the fun, events, holiday lights, and decorations a girl could ask for. Yet I was saddened and a bit disillusioned by the whole thing. As I sat there in the silence of the moment, I felt a nudging from the Holy Spirit to open my Bible. If I were honest with you, I would tell you that I had not spent much time in His word and even less time sitting at His feet. I had gotten busy with all the doing of the season: buying the gifts, decorating the house, leading teams at church, going to the Christmas pageants for my littles, taking our family to the holiday parades, caroling at the nursing home, and the list goes on and on. You see, my heart had been captured by the spirit of the season, but not by the Spirit of God.

I wonder if you can relate to this. Because I think it's safe to say that, as we approach the holiday season, we are collectively looking forward to an increased awareness of hope, peace, love, and joy. We love the notion of peace on earth, goodwill toward men, sharing the love by giving gifts, and finding an extra portion of peace and hope in the hustle and bustle of the season. But then, once the season has passed, we often find ourselves feeling empty and longing for more. Jesus wants us to know that there is a joy that offers a much deeper meaning than that of the holiday season. One that fills us completely and overflows into the lives of others.

He is trying to tell us in John 15 that joy is found, not in a season, but rather in the practice of dwelling with the Savior. Joy that satisfies is a reward for doing the work of abiding in His presence. You see, true joy is rooted in choosing to dwell in His word and presence. The key word here is "dwell." We are used to everything in this world that satisfies very quickly, but not deeply. We think we want a microwave version of joy. But that version leaves us empty just a short time later. Instead, He is asking us to dig into His word, to put in the hard work, to seek Him out and sit with Him.

Prayer

Dear Lord,

Please forgive us for not seeking you out above all else and for substituting time in your word with things that do not satisfy. This advent season, we ask that you would help us not to miss the dwelling with our Savior because of all of the doing, so that His joy may be made complete in us.

Good News of Great Joy
By Lane M. Arnold

Here in the dark, the soft bleating of sheep and the steady rhythm of breathing among us shepherds keeping watch, sound peacefully quiet. The stars glimmer like promises whispered across the heavens. I struggle to stay awake. I nod off, weary from the worry of caring for sheep.

I startle, awakened by a sky ablaze with brilliant light. I blink and then rub my eyes. I shiver, arms covered in goosebumps, yet not from the night air. I jostle my brother, an elbow in his side. The other shepherds shudder, cover their faces—all our hearts pound. An angel stands before us in the field and declares, "Do not be afraid. I bring you good news of great joy that will be for all the people."

Good News. Great Joy. For all people. Even for me? Even for us nobodies, who smell of sheep and sleep under the open sky? As suddenly as they appeared, the angels leave.

We rub our eyes. Was that a dream? "No. No. No!" One after another of my friends nods in agreement. "Let's go. Let's go now."

We take off running. Usually, we are gruff, yet tonight, laughter rings loud as we clutch our cloaks and sprint across the fields into Bethlehem. We find a newborn baby in a manger surrounded by dear Mary and kind Joseph. We've waited so long for the Messiah, the Anointed One. Joy! Joy! Joy!

A hush settles over us. Every eye glistens in happy tears. That we, ordinary unseen shepherds, should be the first to behold this Glorious One. Oh, my. Oh, my. Oh, my.

We cannot hold back our joy. It overflows. It refuses to be contained. It's the thick mystery of Presence. God has come near. Joy found us. In the dark. In the ordinary. In the mess. In the monotony of sheep and sleepless nights.

We tremble with wonder. We cannot contain the delight. We dash, shouting through the village and the fields, "Behold! Behold! Behold! Christ has come." Joy's alive in a manger.

Sometimes I feel like those shepherds—ordinary, unseen, just trying to make it through another long night. Bills to pay, work to do, worries that nibble at the edges of peace. And yet, in these aging years, as a caregiver, as a provider, the pounding in my heart questions how I'll make it in these dark stretches. I sit in the weariness, nodding off, when along comes God. He sprinkles joy.

Advent interrupts the ordinary to declare: God has come near. What does your dark field look like? A sick child? A kitchen sink full of dirty dishes? An aging parent? A job loss? An overwhelming diagnosis? What surrounds you with nagging weariness?

Let this Advent be a moment that interrupts the ordinary with extraordinary joy. Let God's gaze of lavish love warm the cold and weary places. The same God who filled the night sky with song for shepherds still fills our hearts with quiet assurance. You are seen, you are loved, and joy is possible—even here, even now. God has come near. Joy! Joy! Joy!

Prayer

Lord, awaken in us the joy of the shepherds—the wonder of Your nearness and the uncontainable boldness. When the night feels long, remind us that light has already come. Teach us to live as one who has heard the Good News of Great Joy, and to carry that Joy wherever we go. Amen.

There's Still Joy Amidst the Uncertainty

By Stephanie Mora

It was a cold December night when my mother and I arrived at my grandparents' home with a few suitcases in hand and our bunny, Pepper, in tow. Due to a dangerous environment, we had to leave our home immediately, and in the blink of an eye, we found ourselves homeless. After a hectic week of staying at an Airbnb, my grandpa invited us to stay with them. This definitely was not the ideal way to spend the Advent season, but we were thankful to have somewhere to go while we found a new home.

Sitting on the edge of the bed, I stared at my grandmother's closet, and a wave of sadness swept over me as I saw her unused dresses just hanging. I closed my eyes and let the emotions and memories take hold. My grandmother had suffered a stroke a few months back, and she wasn't the same anymore. She went from being a talkative and active woman who loved dressing up to a quiet, frail woman whose short-term memory was declining rapidly. The pain and heaviness in my grandfather's eyes were palpable when he confided in me how hard life had been ever since. The year was filled with hospital visits, grief, and uncertainty- lots of uncertainty.

But something strange caught me off guard as I felt God softly whisper to my heart that I was gifted the opportunity to spend time with my grandparents and help them in one of their biggest times of need. Despite the chaos I was going through, I started to feel little snippets of joy weaving into this season. Pepper kept my grandpa company in the morning while he exercised, and both my mom and I were there to pray with him when Grandma had unexpected trips to the hospital. As days went by, I realized I was forming new memories with them, creating a stronger bond that otherwise might not have happened if we hadn't been forced out of our home.

In these moments, I thought of when Mary was visited by the shepherds and the joy she must have felt when Jesus was born. The events leading up to the birth of Jesus were not easy, and the journey must have felt unclear at times. However, Mary was able to ponder these moments and treasure them in her heart. She could cling to joy not because circumstances were perfect, but because as she carried Jesus in her womb, He was with her through it all.

This Advent season was a strong reminder for me of how joy wasn't just in laughter and happy, carefree moments. It was staying rooted in the Word and the promises of God despite the uncertainty and sorrow. And when we don't know how the future will pan out, like Mary, we can hold new memories and Jesus in our hearts.

Prayer

Heavenly Father, the author of our life, You know that there will be moments where uncertainty and the unknown will loom over our heads like a dark cloud. We thank You because our joy isn't found in the absence of heartaches and trials but in Your faithfulness and Word. During the inevitable storms, help our faith remain strong.

Joy in the Waiting
By Sherri S. Autrey

It's not easy to be still.

To wait.

To cease the striving.

It's not easy to slow down.

To pause.

To stop the rushing.

Most of us are impatient people accustomed to instant gratification. We live in a world that moves at supersonic speed, and we often fear that if we hesitate, we'll be left behind. Or, if we're honest, maybe we're afraid of hearing God speak. And so, we wrestle in the tension between stillness with Christ and constantly pushing forward in our own strength.

In all the hurriedness, we've mistakenly believed that joy only comes as a reward for our relentless self-efforts. We think we'll finally grasp contentment when our circumstances are perfect, and our agendas are successfully executed. But God's joy defies human logic, and it's not dependent on what we do or how much we achieve. Instead, when we pause and trust Him, He brings joy in the middle of our waiting. And His plan always unfolds at just the right moment. However, if we don't slow down and pay attention, we will miss the miracle.

That's what happened in Bethlehem on the night Jesus was born. The town was overcrowded with people returning for the census, and they were busy as they hurried to find places to stay. Their clothes were dusty from traveling, and their children were probably hungry and tired. It didn't appear to be the time or the place for the long-awaited Messiah to enter the world. But God had other plans!

He sent Jesus into our brokenness, and it happened in His perfect timing. Yet, most of the people in Bethlehem missed that sacred moment. They weren't looking for joy in the "here-and-now" because they had allowed their circumstances to dictate the condition of their hearts.

Jesus arrived in the most unexpected way, but the miracle of that first Christmas was not only about His virgin birth and God's gift of redemption, but it was also about His magnificent joy come to earth for all mankind. This is the type of joy that made wise men bow and shepherds break out in worship! And this is the joy that still comes today - despite our busyness, our heartaches, and our struggles.

During this Advent season, may we linger in His presence without being held captive by agendas or derailed by distractions. Let's not miss the miracle of the Lord's divine joy at work in our hearts as we pause to be still before Him. Because in the waiting, there is joy. Joy without limits or restrictions. Joy in knowing He is coming and that His plans are always perfect. Joy in trusting His promises and experiencing His redeeming grace.

In our quietness and stillness, may we discover Christ anew. And even amid noise and activity, may we pause long enough to realize the true gift of Christmas, because there is always joy in the waiting.

Prayer

Lord, we pause in the stillness of this moment to praise you for your supernatural joy. Forgive us for when we barge ahead instead of waiting for you. And thank you that no matter what we're going through, our hearts can always rejoice as we trust in you. Amen.

When Joy Finds Us in the Letting Go
By Leighann Rechtin

For fifteen years, I poured my heart into a job I truly loved. I imagined I would retire there. It felt secure, familiar, meaningful, and, in many ways, part of who I was. But over time, a quiet restlessness began to stir. I couldn't quite name it, but something in me felt unsettled, like a lamp flickering in a room that once felt bright. Still, I kept going. I told myself that loyalty mattered more than change, that perhaps this was just a season to push through.

I felt numb. Like I was standing in that cold night - bleary and weary - with the shepherds on that hillside long ago. Then, this past May, everything changed. Without warning, the job I thought I'd keep until retirement was gone. I was laid off.

Looking back now, I see that God didn't remove something from me; He was making space for me. I had been holding tightly to what was comfortable, afraid to imagine something new. In His mercy, God allowed an ending so that I could experience a different kind of beginning.

In Luke 2:10, the angel declares, "Fear not, for behold, I bring you good news of great joy that will be for all the people." The shepherds weren't looking for joy. They were simply keeping watch, doing their ordinary work in the dark. Yet joy found them first, breaking through their night with light and promise.

That's how God's joy often comes. Not when everything is certain, but when we're watching, waiting, and willing to be surprised. My layoff, which felt like a great loss, has become a season of renewal. I've discovered that joy doesn't always come wrapped in comfort. Sometimes it's hidden in surrender, in trust, in letting go of what no longer fits the person God is shaping us to become.

This Advent, as I reflect on my journey, I realize joy was never lost; it was simply waiting for me on the other side of obedience. It came quietly, in God's timing, reminding me that His plans are never to harm but to give hope and a future.

We often confuse joy with happiness, expecting it to look like glittering perfection and constant cheer. But Advent reminds us that joy can come quietly, lying in a manger, on a cold night. It can coexist with weariness, grief, or longing because it is rooted in the nearness of God, not the neatness of life.

Joy, at its core, is about presence. Christ's presence that meets us where we are and reminds us that we are never alone. It is a gift that often arrives in stillness, in surrender, in the in-between places of waiting.

So if joy feels distant this Advent, take heart. You don't have to chase it. Simply make room for the One who brings it. He will come to you, just as surely as He came to Bethlehem that night. Let your heart listen for joy's quiet knock. It is already on its way. Joy isn't found by holding on. It finds us when we open our hands.

Prayer

Lord Jesus, thank You for being the kind of Savior who meets us in our endings as well as our beginnings. When life shifts and plans fall apart, help us trust that You are making room for new joy. Let Your presence light our way as we wait and watch for You this Advent. Amen.

The Joy Within
By Julie W. Smith

From the beginning of scripture, we see God as a loving father, Jesus the Son, and the Holy Spirit. When sin entered the world, a plan was formed to offer forgiveness to man. Throughout the Old Testament God tells man that there will come a time when Christ will enter the world and bring salvation.

Can you imagine the anticipation? Year after year. Wondering. Waiting for the Messiah to come. King of Kings and Prince of Peace. Jesus chose not to come to earth in a blaze of glory but as a tiny baby. Wonder how God felt watching His Son become a lowly human. Helpless. Longing to protect Him as a father would.

God sent angels to announce his birth not to kings but to humble shepherds out in the field. They were filled with awe and joy as they hurried to Bethlehem to see Jesus. The shepherds bowed and worshipped the baby who lay before them.

God's love for us came down that Christmas Day. His only Son was lying in a feed trough. Jesus was used to much grander accommodations; yet, this is what He chose.

On Christmas Eve, my daddy would read the Christmas story to prepare our hearts for the celebration of Christ's birth. Even though I've heard and read the story many times before, it still fills me with awe and wonder.

A father's love for his children leads him to sometimes become a child again, particularly on Christmas morning. Sitting on the floor playing games. Riding his children horseback and laughing. Helping them to ride a bicycle for the first time. He was always there by our side to support us and keep us from falling. God loves us like that. He has promised to never leave us. He is always with us no matter what the circumstances are. He doesn't leave us to walk through them alone.

The verse I chose to be the theme for this devotional is not one you would normally choose in relation to the Christmas story– Hebrews 12:2. It's because of His birth, life and death that we have the joy of salvation. He had to be born in order to die for our sins. He loved us that much!

Growing up as a child and even after becoming an adult, Christmas was a special time of celebration. We would gather at my parents' or grandparents' house. Spending time together as a family was paramount.

My father was a big part of our lives. His love for his family was only surpassed by his love for God. The joy of the Lord radiated through him. He passed away in September.

This Christmas will be the first one without him. It's bittersweet, but because of the baby in the manger and his death on the cross, I know he is rejoicing with his Savior. I have the assurance that I will see him again!

Yes, this year may bring sadness and tears, but there's a joy deep within that knows my dad is okay. He is healed and loving heaven. All because of a baby in a manger.

Prayer

Heavenly Father, thank you for sending Jesus to show how much you love us. Fill our hearts with joy during this Christmas season and let it spill over to the lives of others. For the broken-hearted, we ask for comfort. We pray in the name of Jesus. Amen.

The Source of True Joy
By Patti Selvey

How is your heart today, sweet friend? This busy season of preparing our homes for hospitality with decorations to install, menus to plan, gifts to buy, and activities to attend can leave us distracted, depleted, and disenfranchised. The 'fun' can leave us frazzled. The 'hustle and bustle' can 'hustle the bustle' right out of us if we aren't intentional.

Perhaps you can relate to my past empty disappointment on December 26th when reflecting on the hurried pace and thought, "I can't believe it's over already"? Maybe for you, your heart feels lonely and heavy this season. The cultural images of the 'perfect holiday' are glaring and hurtful as you carry the pain of difficulty. Loss, grief, broken dreams, and heartache weigh you down. You are ready to get past the world's holiday dazzle and say, "At last, I'm glad it's over."

Or perhaps you find yourself just 'showing up' – unaware of hurriedness or hurt–just going through the motions, a tad numb and merely existing. The seasonal win will be surviving into the new year. There may be some fun moments to be had in the days ahead, but overall, you are uninvested and disinterested. When the season ends, your reaction will have a twinge of 'I made it through. It was just another day".

Maybe you, like me, can honestly relate to each of these states at different points. Which begs the question: for a season that is outwardly depicted as 'merry and bright', what do we do when our spiritual hearts are overwhelmed? Downcast? Unfeeling? In this broken world, where does true joy come from?

Scripture tells us in Psalm 16:11 that God is the one who makes the path of life known to us. He alone is the one who fills us with true joy as we enter his presence. And there in his presence is everlasting pleasure—true delight to our hearts that lasts forever.

This challenges us to seek the lasting and complete joy promised when we are in relationship with Jesus Christ as our Lord and Savior. This joy is marked with peace and contentment beyond life's circumstances. It is not temporary happiness based upon flurry and festivities, nor just enduring through another day. It is genuine everlasting joy within our spirits because of who Jesus is, his role in our lives, and the complete work that he achieved on the cross to save us.

The world and its trappings do not know or offer this kind of pure joy. As our verse states, it is only found on the path of life God makes known to us and brings delight to our hearts starting now, despite current conditions.

So, I'm asking again, "How's your heart today, sweet friend?" As Advent continues, may we be people who prepare our hearts more than we prepare our houses and calendars. Let's be intentional to slow down and seek the presence of Christ. Let's remember the true gift of the season: Jesus, lowering himself to earth as a baby, born in a dark cave housing smelly animals in the little town of Bethlehem. No glitz, no glam. Simply a meager manger filled with the most enormous gift of God's love, Jesus.

May Jesus's arrival and the hope of his promised second coming (the second Advent!) be the source of true joy in our hearts and the meaning of our celebrations this season.

Prayer

Gracious Father,

You are faithful. We pause to be in your presence, Jesus—the source of true joy. Remind us often through your Holy Spirit to lift our gaze up to you and think on heavenly things during the busyness, hurt, and mundanity of life. Help us prepare our hearts during this special season of celebrating the gift of you, Jesus. Amen.

Joy in Suffering
By Elizabeth A. Prentiss

When Job endured the kind of misery few of us can fathom, he was defeated, desperate for relief. When three men entered the furnace, all hope appeared to be lost. When a lowly carpenter from Galilee faced unthinkable pain and torment, there was great suffering. But God wasn't finished yet. Joy came with the morning, and even with the mourning. And what a glorious joy it was!

As Paul spoke of rejoicing in trials, he must have thought beyond his personal experiences, which were substantial, and remembered these examples from history and countless other times God brought His children through great suffering.

Over the course of seven years, I lost 10 family members (including two sweet sisters and my dear dad), saw several other loved ones live through near-death crises, and faced family and personal traumas worthy of a daytime drama storyline.

You may think I have little to celebrate this season. Too much suffering to be thankful or joyful in this life. It's not an unreasonable assumption.

But God. Without Him, I could not have survived this battleground. Without Him, I would have lost hope long ago. With God, I found joy in suffering. Despite the absolute heartbreak, I have more joy now than ever before.

Suffering teaches us to look up. To look at the gifts we are given, at the miracles all around us. Most of all to look to the One who never left us, despite the loss, the flames, the pain.

Paul taught us to "count it all joy", not from a place of comfort and privilege, but from a place of trust, endurance, fortitude, and determination, even in the midst of shipwrecks, persecution, and imprisonment.

Job knew he could trust God, even if He slayed him. Shadrach, Meshach, and Abednego knew they were not alone in the flames. Jesus knew we were worth saving, worth the ultimate sacrifice.

I know there is great joy in the LORD, even when everything else falls away. When we have nothing to hold on to, no strength, no net, all we can do is cry out to Jesus. In those desperate, aching moments, the certainty of the Father's hands carrying us through causes an immeasurable joy that cannot be replicated by anything in the human world. Only by the steady goodness of God can we experience true, unshakable joy, and it is through great suffering that this joy is amplified to its fullest reality.

Fellow believer, this season may we be reminded of the weight of God's love for us, the cost of that love, and the pure joy He offers.

And for those of us who may be facing the holidays while experiencing grief, you have my heart, but most of all, you have God's heart. Lean into Him. Hard as it may be, thank Him for the pain and trust that He will bring you through it, knowing there is joy on the other side of suffering.

Prayer

Father, thank you for your great compassion for your children as they face the difficulties and struggles of this life. The gift of your Son is the greatest source of joy and peace we could ask for. As we celebrate Christ's birth, let those with broken hearts be comforted by your promise of joy and healing. In Jesus' name, Amen.

Follow the Star to Joy
By Elizabeth P. Buttimer

As a child, I remember the anticipation that I felt every day when I opened another window on the Advent calendar. The Christmas calendar told the story of the baby born in a manger who would grow up to be Immanuel, God with us. The calendar itself, printed in rich saturated colors, reminded me of the crimson, sapphire, emerald, gold, and other shades featured in our church's stained-glass windows. Those vibrant colors were fit for a King.

With the approach of Christmas, I always sensed that there was something sacred coming. A blessing was arriving for me, and for everyone. The miracle of God's love was made manifest as a newborn Savior and would again be celebrated anew. As Mary had done, I pondered the wonder of it all in my heart.

The excitement of the season filled me with expectation. Just as Mary had expected a baby to be born, I awaited the arrival of Jesus' birthday. Marking each day took me one step closer until "the time came for her to give birth" (Luke 2:6).

Opening the last door on Christmas Eve made the waiting complete. The scene revealed a newborn nestled in a stable with the star's light casting a bright luster overall. Mary, Joseph, the shepherds, the animals in the silent night, and the star captured the moment that changed eternity. There above them were angels singing and glorifying God. Centuries after that instant, I was there, too—a child kneeling with the shepherds. I was filled with joy and awed by the majesty within that miracle.

The Wise Men followed the star across difficult terrain as they searched for the prophesied young King. Their determination never waned. In time, the Magi came and beheld the precious child with His mother. Overwhelmed with joy, they worshipped Him. The Wise Men opened both the treasure of their hearts and the gifts they had brought Him.

That simple Advent calendar had vividly depicted the birth of our Lord. The joy that filled that night could be seen in a child's face full of hope, awe, and wonder.

As adults, however, we often let responsibilities and duties crowd out the simple joys that surround childhood Christmases. Our focus shifts from the manger, to the mundane, from glory to "got to", everlasting to everyday, and from a crown to a kitchen.

In the days that build up to Christmas, we never stop until our to-do list is completed. There's only one problem. The to-do list never ends. We keep adding to it, one thing after another. Advent becomes a race. Can we finish our to-do list before Christmas?

Creating meaningful memories matters for us all, but especially children and families. We, however, often focus on what we think children want under the tree or in their stockings, rather than on what children truly crave. Love of family, positive attention, respect, and togetherness can be better than anything else. Electronics become outdated, toys break, fashions go out of style, and shiny cars dent or tarnish.

This Christmas, I wish you a full measure of joy undiluted by the world's emphasis on temporal things. I hope that, as the Wise Men, you too will follow the Star of Bethlehem.

Prayer

Almighty Father, thank you for the miracle of Christmas and the joy that awaits us this Holy Season. Lord, help us to follow the Star of Bethlehem despite the worldly distractions that would keep us from focusing on You. Please open our hearts to receive the greatest gift of all, Your love. In Jesus name, Amen.

Reflections on Love

Love Never Fails
By Janell Rardon

As we trekked through Fort Hatteras, love was the last thing on my mind. I was dripping sweat, my leg was bleeding, and I felt hopelessly lost.

Just thirty minutes earlier, my husband and I were on a lovely beach walk along the coastline of our happy place, Hatteras Island. South winds blew softly, soft waves rushed over my feet, and the timing of the tides for beach combing was perfect. I felt the cares of this world washing over me like the waves.

At that moment of perfect peace, my husband looked to the right and saw the sound. That's the distinct glory of the Outer Banks of North Carolina, particularly Hatteras Island, on the east is the ocean and on the west is the sound. Suddenly, he lights up!

"Look, we are so close to the sound." He suggests we go on a little adventure and take the path less travelled.

Hesitant at first, I took a minute. "Are you sure it's safe?" I ask.

"Of course," he answers. "How many years have we been coming here? I know this beach like the back of my hand." With over forty years of experience, he convinced me to trust him.

Everything was going fine, until we reached a point where the beach we were walking on disappeared. Ahead of us was an impasse of water, about 15 feet wide and two feet deep.

"I don't know about this," I said.

"We'll be fine. Trust me," he smiled.

Once again, I took a minute.

"Do you want to turn back?" he asked.

Everything in me wanted to say yes, but then this little whisper rose, "You've got this. Keep moving forward." He stretched out his hand and together we waded through the water.

When we got to the other side, we found ourselves in thick reeds, deep mud, and finally, in a forest-like, wooded area. We had to climb under thickets with very large thorns, and within minutes, saw no path forward.

"Hold on," my husband said. "Let me get my bearings."

I could tell he was lost, but trusted his honed navigational instincts, so I paused.

And I prayed.

Suddenly, out of seeming nowhere, a couple appeared from the other side of the woods.

"Hello," they said. I noticed the man was wearing a Jesus t-shirt and smiled. To this day, I believe they were angels.

"Are you walking through here without shoes?" the man asked. "You know this is the old Fort Hatteras. We come here once a year to look for old cannonballs."

"Can you please help us get out of here?" I winced. They sweetly showed us the way and continued their adventure.

I wish I could report that we found our way back to the beach quickly, but it took some time. We still had to push through more thorny thickets, cross burning hot sand, and walk almost 2.0 miles to our beach camp.

About a mile in, Rob looked at me and said, "I can't believe you aren't raging at me right now. I'm so sorry."

Honestly, I couldn't believe it either, but I remembered that little whisper.

This trek felt like a living, breathing word picture for the unfamiliar territory, filled with obstacles and challenges, we were facing in our life. I recognized that God was inviting us to a deeper understanding of His incomparable love.

Prayer

Father, this Advent season, remind me that You are always with me. You guide me to safety. When I am weak, worried, and weary, help me know that You are close and that Your love never fails (1 Corinthians 13:8).

Rerouted Love
By Crystal Olp

This is not how it should be! That thought lodged in my mind on that icy December afternoon, just days before Christmas. It had been a stressful 48 hours as my brave, beautiful daughter worked to bring my grandson into this world. These thoughts were like a song stuck on repeat, reaching deeper into my heart and attempting to smother the truth. Paralysis loomed as I stood in the hospital room holding my precious newborn grandson, knowing I would soon hand him over to his amazing "chosen" family. This was not how it was supposed to be! Yet many circumstances led to my daughter's decision, and I was extremely proud of her. Her courage, strength, determination, and love for him wove themselves into every action. Still, it did not ease the pain in my heart for both myself and my beloved daughter.

She had chosen a lovely family who loved Jesus, each other, and people. He would be blessed by godly parents and attentive brothers. He would grow up with cousins, know his story, and learn how God was in it. We would occasionally see him, and he would know his biological mother, hopefully with an open relationship. He would grow up deeply loved by all of us. We had peace that this was right, yet those intruding thoughts remained.

Days later, Christmas Eve came with no fanfare—no decorations, gifts, or big meal. As I lay in bed chatting with God, I felt Him whisper, "This is how I felt as I laid my Son into Mary's womb." I froze. What? I had never pondered that sending Jesus was not His original plan. He chose what was best for creation, placing His only Son on this planet. He loved us that much. He willingly gave us Jesus, choosing His earthly parents just as my daughter chose her son's. He rerouted Jesus' life as a gift for humanity.

Just as we know the end of Jesus's story, God graciously revealed glimpses of ours. Over 50 years ago, the great-grandparents of both families had been friends at the same church in another city. A black-and-white photo even shows my grandson's adoptive great-grandparents waving goodbye to his biological great-grandparents as they left to serve in Africa. None of them could have known that moment would later bring solace to this grandma's aching heart. My daughter chose the family through a random agency with three photo books—but God knew. What a gift that we can trust His rerouted plans.

In this Advent season, pause and ponder the gift of a baby sent to walk with us. God's rerouted plan can always be trusted. He loves us!

Prayer

O God of light and promise, in this Advent season, we wait with longing hearts. We thank You for courage born of love, for the gift of new life, and for Christ, Your Son, our hope and salvation. Teach us to trust Your timing, to rejoice in Your mercy, Your rerouted plans, and to rest in Your unfailing love. Amen.

The True Grit of Christmas
By Julie D Davis

For as long as I can remember, Christmas has been my favorite time of year. To me, it was always a celebration of God's incredible love—He sent His only Son for each one of us, even for me! I've always cherished the lights, the music, and the quiet wonder of imagining that first Christmas night—the love and awe Mary must have felt as she held her Son, the one who would change the world.

But for many years, my expectations of the "perfect" family Christmas never seemed to come true. Family dynamics, church events, time pressures, financial strain, or disappointments always left me feeling let down. What I thought should be the happiest season often became a season of frustration.

Then one year, God gently shifted my perspective. He reminded me that the heart of Christmas has never depended on perfect gatherings, gifts, or circumstances. The true meaning of Christmas is this: God loves us so deeply that—even if we were the only ones on earth—He still would have sent His Son. Jesus came as a humble baby, lived to show us God's love, and ultimately gave His life on the cross so that all who accept His gift of salvation will have eternal life with Him.

That realization changed everything. The decorations, the presents, and the family traditions are all wonderful blessings, but they are not the heart of Christmas. The greatest gift is Jesus Himself—God with us—and the assurance of His love that remains with me every day of the year.

So now, whether my family can gather in celebration or not, Christmas is always alive in my heart. And that truth brings peace and joy no matter the season. "For unto you is born this day in the city of David a Savior, who is Christ the Lord" (Luke 2:11). Here is a question to consider: What expectations or distractions might be keeping you from fully embracing the true meaning of Christmas this year?

Prayer

Lord, thank You for the gift of Your Son, Jesus. Help me to remember that the heart of Christmas is not in perfect traditions, but in Your perfect love. Teach me to celebrate You above all else, share Your love with others, and carry the joy of Your presence in my heart each day. Amen.

Love in the Little Moments
By Laura Lee Pettit

There's something sacred about quiet moments—when the noise dims, and we find space to reflect. Mary, young and likely overwhelmed, still made room in her heart to treasure what God was doing. Amidst uncertainty, discomfort, and unexpected circumstances, she held onto the truth: Love had come near.

There was a period of time—over several Christmas seasons—when my nephew Joshua was a toddler, and I would pull out our kid-friendly nativity set. As I told the story of the first Christmas, Joshua carefully placed each figure—shepherds, angels, animals, wise men, Joseph, Mary, and finally, baby Jesus—into the little plastic stable. The joy on his face was pure, his focus completely on baby Jesus.

That simple ritual was more than a moment of innocence. It was sacred. A child remembering the Child. And I, watching Joshua, was reminded that love is best understood not by grandeur but in simplicity—a truth easy to forget in the busyness of the season.

We decorate, plan, shop, and schedule until our hearts are too full to make room for the very One we are meant to celebrate. Love doesn't need elaborate circumstances to show up. Jesus was born in a stable, not a palace. He came not for comfort, but to bring comfort. God's love entered the world humbly—unwrapped and unexpected, yet unstoppable.

One afternoon, as I sat at my kitchen table reading and writing, the sun suddenly broke through the clouds. A single beam of light shone directly on me. The shadows sharpened, and I could see even the smudges on my glasses. It was such a distinct, beautiful moment that I paused, overwhelmed. It felt like God whispering, "I see you. I am here. My love surrounds you."

That is Christmas. Not always loud, not always festive, but filled with moments—if we're willing to ponder them—where God meets us with His love.

The love I feel for Joshua is real, deep, and fierce. Yet it doesn't compare to the love God has for him—or for me, or for you. God's love is sacrificial, personal, and boundless. It doesn't demand perfectly decorated trees or spectacularly lit homes. It asks only for a willing heart.

When Mary sang her praise in the first chapter of Luke, it was more than poetic worship – it was a bold declaration of God's love in action. Her song wasn't wrapped in extravagance or complexity. It was simple, yet powerful. Mary rejoices not just because she is carrying a baby, but because God sees the humble, lifts the lowly, feeds the hungry, and keeps His promises – all flowing from a heart of perfect love.

Like Mary, ponder love. Like Joshua, delight in the story. And like the shepherds, go and share the good news: Love has come. Love is here. Love will never leave. Here are some questions to consider: What would it look like to make room in your heart and schedule for God's love this Christmas? In what small or unexpected places have you recently seen signs of God's presence? How can you reflect God's love to someone in your life who might need it this season?

Prayer

Lord, help us to pause this Advent and treasure what You are doing in our lives. Open our eyes so we do not miss the simple, sacred moments where Your love breaks through. Thank You for the gift of Jesus—Your love in the flesh. May we receive Him fully and reflect His love to others.

Love that Lasts Forever
By Marla Rae Wartell

Several years ago, before tragedy struck and flames swept through the beautiful Notre Dame Cathedral, I had the chance to walk through its doors. My son, who was stationed in Germany at the time, accompanied me. He wanted to celebrate my fiftieth birthday in a most memorable way. Paris was just the place, and Notre Dame was certainly on the list of our must-see places.

I'll always remember the moment we crossed the ancient cathedral threshold. Stained glass windows offered dim light, and the glow of candles and chandeliers cast warmth into the dark spaces. The air was hushed, almost as if the building itself was breathing a sacred silence. In that instant, I felt the overwhelming presence and love of God.

It wasn't just the grandeur of the historic building that moved me—it was the awareness that the same God who inspired generations to build this cathedral was the same God who was meeting me there, pouring out His love in a way that felt both eternal and deeply personal.

Psalm 107:1 tells us, "Oh give thanks to the Lord, for he is good for his steadfast love endures forever!" God's love isn't limited by time, place, or circumstance. The same love that spoke creation into being, the same love that sent Jesus to the cross for you and me, is the very same love that reaches into your life today. His love has no expiration date.

Walking through Notre Dame reminded me of that truth. The cathedral stood for centuries, weathering wars, revolutions, and even fire. But as beautiful as it was, even stone and stained glass can crumble. Only God's love remains unshaken through all generations. From before time began, to the building of that cathedral, to this very moment in your life, His love has never once failed.

Cathedrals may fall, but God's love never does. His love was with the generations before us, it's with us now, and it will be with those who come after us. The same God who stirred generations to build such a masterpiece was the same God stirring my heart that day. His love felt endless, timeless, eternal. Sharing those moments with my son was a precious gift I'll always treasure.

Maybe right now you're walking through a season of uncertainty. Life may feel unstable, as though the walls around you could collapse at any moment. You might be facing changes, losses, or questions you don't have answers for. Here's the good news: you are held by a love that will not fail you. God's love is the anchor in your storm, the light in your darkness, the steady hope when everything else shifts and changes.

So today, take a moment to pause and give thanks. Thank Him for the ways He has shown His goodness in your life. Thank Him for loving you with a love that never runs out. And if you've been holding back, unsure if you can trust Him with your future, let today be the day you surrender your heart fully to the One who loves you most.

Prayer

Lord, thank You for Your never-ending love. Thank You that in every season of life, You remain faithful. Today, I surrender anything that holds me back. Help me to trust You with my whole heart and to rest in the truth that Your love for me endures forever. Amen.

In Focus: Keeping Our Eyes on Jesus

By Brianna Barrett

This past summer, our family took a road trip along the iconic Historic Route 66. During the trip, we stopped at dozens of places so I could take pictures. When I photograph things, I always have to make sure my lens is focused on the object or landscape I'm trying to capture; otherwise, my picture will be blurry. As I was going through the pictures creating a scrapbook, I noticed several photos that weren't in focus. It reminded me how—especially during the holidays—it is easy to lose focus on what's important. Between juggling schedules, finances, splitting time among everyone, buying gifts and baking cookies, and watching the amount of calories I consume to fit into my post-holiday clothes, my focus easily becomes blurred. When life becomes chaotic and busy, our focus easily blurs, and when we're just going through the motions to check items off a list, we can forget what we should be focused on.

Jesus gives us the most important commandment in Mark 12:30-31, "'And you shall love the Lord your God with all your heart and with all your soul and with all your mind and with all your strength.' The second is this: 'You shall love your neighbor as yourself.' There is no other commandment greater than these." When we focus on loving God, loving others, and loving ourselves, we can be obedient to God and grow our faith. When we focus on loving the ones surrounding us—meeting them where they are—our focus is on doing good for others, reflecting the image of Christ.

Maybe during the holidays, focusing on growing your faith isn't at the top of your list. Other things have taken your attention and focus. As another year ends and a new year quickly approaches, we make resolutions, lists of things we are going to change and do better, and things we are going to eliminate from our lives. Start today. Instead of trying to win the argument with your relatives, even the ones who really rub you the wrong way, share your faith and the fruits of the Spirit with them. Shower them with love and kindness. Even if you have different views, love them anyway.

Jesus calls us in John 13:34-35, giving a new commandment, "'love one another: just as I have loved you, you also are to love one another. By this all people will know that you are my disciples, if you have love for one another.'" Jesus didn't tell us to focus on the people who are like us to love; He said, Love each other as He loved. When we keep our focus on Jesus, we can reflect His love to others. Don't you want people to clearly see Jesus in you instead of a blurred image? When we focus on Jesus, we grow our faith, drawing near to Jesus and being obedient to His will, not our own. I encourage you today to grow your faith more and to focus on Jesus. To do so, you must be obedient to His commands.

This holiday season: love God, love others, love yourself, just as Jesus commanded us—with all our hearts, minds, souls, and strength. I want people to feel loved when they are around me, and to clearly see Jesus through my words and actions so that they may feel Christ's love and peace.

Prayer

Lord, thank you for this reminder to help me refocus on the real meaning of Christmas. May my thoughts and actions align with Your will. I pray others would see You through me. Thank you, Lord. In Jesus' name. Amen.

Echoes of Our Savior's Love
By Jena Beecher

I stood at the open door, my eyes wide and mouth gaping. At age eight, I felt like I was peeking at secret Christmas gifts while my mother met with the choir director. Paralyzed, I gazed upon the most beautiful Christmas ornaments and wondered, 'Who created these?' I was stunned to learn it was my very own great-aunt, who sat alone in the same seat on the same pew each Sunday.

Many assumed Nell was a widow who lived with her sister. In truth, abandoned by her husband, she supported her disabled sister with earnings as a florist's assistant. Despite many disappointments, Nell never complained. Just like the symbols in our church's stained-glass windows, each flower, wreath, and garland held its own special meaning in retelling the story of Jesus' birth long ago.

I most adored the Advent wreath. Set upon a tall stand with purple, pink, and white pillar candles, lit each Sunday between Thanksgiving and Christmas. Excitement grew with each candle lighting. As a congregation, we reflected on His divine love. I'm not sure many of us children were reflecting on His love, but the echoes of our Savior's love were present. Over time, I grew to cherish this time of reflection even more than Nell's Christmas greenery.

In Luke's record of Jesus' birth, echoes of divine love are present. Pregnancy for a young, unmarried girl, especially in a small village, meant living in social disgrace. God sent a messenger angel to declare she would be with child, conceived by the Holy Spirit. He also shared that her relative, Elizabeth, was now pregnant and in her sixth month. God not only prepared Mary but also provided support through Elizabeth.

Although we do not know Joseph's first thought when learning of Mary's "situation." Matthew tells us that Joseph considered divorcing Mary. Once again, God sent a messenger, this time while Joseph slept. The angel encouraged Joseph to wed Mary, announcing her baby was the work of the Holy Spirit. He instructed Joseph to name the child Jesus, who would offer salvation from sin. When Joseph woke, he took Mary as his wife.

To be counted for the census, Joseph set out on the arduous journey to Bethlehem with his betrothed. What an uncomfortable journey for already pregnant Mary. On arrival, Bethlehem's homes bulged with travelers. With no space to lodge Mary and Joseph, one innkeeper offered his stable. There, Mary gave birth to Jesus. She wrapped him in strips of cloth to keep him warm. Mary did not have a bed for her baby. Instead, she used a manger intended to hold feed for the animals. Nearby, angels announced the birth to shepherds tending the village's flocks. Surely, many throughout the area heard jubilant echoes of our Savior's love.

Christmas is a time for sharing and receiving God's divine love. Great-aunt Nell used flowers and greenery to tell the story of Jesus' birth, but truly she shared His love for us. You see, God sent his own son, Jesus, to one day die on a cross and resurrect three days later, offering each of us salvation. We need only to believe in Him to have eternal life. When you see an Advent candle or hear choirs singing of Jesus' birth, listen for the echoes of His love. Just as he prepared Mary for baby Jesus, He prepared Nell to share His love through evergreens, poinsettias, and the Rose of Sharon. He is preparing you now for His invitation to receive and experience His love. Pause and listen for echoes of our Savior's love.

Prayer

Father, I struggle to fathom the expanse of your love for me. Gazing at the Advent wreath, my heart ponders the everlasting life that Jesus offers. With the lighting of each Advent candle, direct my reflections on you. Help me recognize the many echoes of your love and open my heart to you. Amen

Loving the Least of These
By Linda J. Dingeldein

She was a tiny slip of a thing. Faded blond hair swept in a disheveled, messy bun, large hoop earrings peeking beneath fallen wisps. A delicate yet weathered face looked up at me. She blinked as I flipped on the outside light. She had been somebody somewhere once. Immediately, her story unraveled. One sentence tumbling over the next, as if she was afraid of being turned away into the dark, winter night.

Tugging my sweater closed, I half-listened, half-prayed as her life unfolded on our doorstep. God, what do you want me to do? Should I invite her in? In the end, her request was simple. "Can I sleep in my van in the church parking lot?"

"Sleep in your car? It's going to snow tonight!" I exclaimed.

"Please!" she pleaded. "Just one night. I'll be gone by morning."

Beyond all sane reasoning, I heard myself offer, "Why don't you stay with us?"

Instantly, her face filled with fear, and she quickly stepped back from the open door. I could tell life had not been kind to her.

Oh, God. Protect her.

So, our winter stranger parked her van on the far side of the church, where tall streetlamps stood as centurion night lights above her.

With a flashlight in hand, I tucked my face against the cold as I went to deliver a thermos of soup, a sandwich, and her only request: ice for her tea.

As I arrived at the door of her van, she put the window down partway. My heart plummeted.

She sat scrunched in the driver's seat, the only empty spot. From floor to ceiling, dashboard to tailgate, there was not an inch of space to see out.

At that moment, I longed to bring her inside, to give her a warm shower and fill her belly with hearty vegetable soup. But here she was in her motel on wheels, her piles of stuff her only companion.

She beamed as I handed over the thermos of soup and the bag of food items. I laughed as I gave her the plastic baggie filled with ice. "Jesus tells us to give a cup of cold water in His name." She laughed with me, her broad smile reaching her tired eyes.

I asked if I could pray for her. One hand on her shoulder and one on my flashlight, I prayed that the angels of the Lord would surround her car and give her sweet sleep. As I prayed, it felt as if a host of angels were sweeping in, taking their rightful place around her.

It was hard to climb into my warm bed knowing that our winter stranger slept in the cold while I slept beneath my thick, warm quilt. Little did I know that my husband's sermon the next morning would be a passage about love and a cup of cold water given in Jesus' name.

Later in the day, when I looked out at the empty, snowy parking lot, I couldn't help but think that ice cubes and vegetable soup were exactly what Christ had in mind when He said, "...as you did it to one of the least of these my brothers, you did it to me" (Matthew 25:40).

Prayer

Jesus,

Give me spiritual eyes that see the needs of those around me. Fill me with a heart that beats with compassion. Guard me from keeping what I should freely give to others. Help me to live a life that overflows with mercy, generosity, and love. Amen

"I Spy..." Bright Eyes!

U.R. Heard

" I spy with my little eye... something RED!" Everyone is now acutely aware of red items near and far away. All involved, trying to locate the one red item that is the chosen focus. What a fun game to play on car trips, when sitting in a waiting room, or even when snuggled on the couch together.

But this game can have a far-reaching influence on our day. "I spy" is a wonderful reminder that we see what we are looking for. My husband had to remind me of this.

Schedules, to-do lists, normal ebb and flow of life had taken a downward turn in my heart. My normally half-full cup was increasingly half-empty. Negatives seemed to be popping prominently into view, blocking my ability to notice the positives around me or to reach out lovingly to anyone.

"Try greeting everyone with encouragement first thing in the morning as they get up," he suggested. I'd like to say that I nominated him for the Best Idea Genius Award (which I should have done!), but his comment was met by a blank stare as I tried to piece together how he had so incredibly missed my point. Or had he?

I was distracted during my reading time the next morning, still arguing in my head the unfeasibility of the idea, when I read in Proverbs 15:30, "The light of the eyes rejoices the heart..." Glad heart. I could definitely use that. Bright eyes can help? Hmm... Bright things do draw our attention. The stars in the night sky. A shaft of light through the trees in the woods. A candle in a dark room. A rainbow refracts the light through the rain droplets.

Maybe there was something to his suggestion that I needed to reconsider. Maybe... greeting each person with a smile, not just on my face but one that brightened my eyes, could set a different tone in our home. And in my heart.

Little feet came scampering into the room. I closed my Bible, purposed to smile brightly into their faces as I greeted them. What a sweet reaction! Their faces lit up and reflected the brightness I had just given.

I reached out and took their hands in mine, whispered excitedly, "Let's go get everyone else out of bed!" We went hand in hand to awaken each sibling. Walking into the bedroom, my focus had changed. I was now actively spying out opportunities to catch that first eye connection so I could greet each one with a welcoming smile and bright eyes. We were all laughing as the little ones snuggled and tickled their older siblings, who were trying to burrow deeper under their covers. We were starting a new bright day!

What began as a good morning greeting then spread into an all-day interaction as I practiced "bright eyes gladden the heart," purposing in my heart to look up with a smile and bright eyes each time someone called my name, entered the room, or walked through the door!

Bright eyes bring a contagious expression of love that infects all you give it to, and, to my surprise, it infected and affected my own heart most of all!

So my husband really does deserve the Best Idea Genius Award! When his suggestion opened my heart to connect with God's Word, it created the best idea!

What is our chosen focus for today? What can we do in a tangible way to demonstrate our love for those around us? How about a game of "I Spy..." and may each of our loved ones find our bright eyes!

Prayer

Father,

Thank You that You are the author and originator of great ideas. Help us to look to You when life gets in the way of what is truly important. Thank You that You can lead us through Your Word and Godly counsel to spy out how to love well the precious ones You have placed in our lives!

When Jesus Didn't Come
By U.R. Heard

Tragedy had struck our home in November. Now we were facing our first Christmas after the car accident. The first Christmas that our son was spending in heaven.

He was celebrating there, but I was struggling here, struggling to remember the reason for Christmas... the beautiful gift of God's love wrapped up in swaddling cloths... announced by Heavenly messengers to some, yet hidden away and unknown to others. Some missed it then. I felt like I was missing it now.

Have you faced a tragedy this year? Or are you desperately seeking God's intervention, anxiously waiting for Him to step in and answer the cries of your heart?

In my grief, I was poring over Scripture. Clinging to promises, to find a steadying hold on His truths. Truths that could stand whatever the future held.

One foundational truth I found is God's love. John 3:16 is the classic verse of God's love. The reason Jesus came. "For God so loved the world, that he gave his only

Son..." I knew it. But there was a questioning riptide in my heart, unseen from the surface, pulling that truth into the depths of doubt. Would He turn away and not step in when I needed Him most if He loved me?

Can we know...Are we still in God's loving hands when life takes an unexpected and tragic turn?

I was amazed by where the answer was found, waiting in a familiar place to meet me and the need of my heart.

I still remember where I was sitting at church. It was the opposite side from where we usually sat. Everything felt a little different. A good place for a new perspective.

As I sat waiting for the service to start, my thoughts once again turned to God's love, wrestling with how allowing tragedy lined up with being loved by Him. I was about to find out.

Opening our Bibles, we turned to John 11. This familiar and beloved passage about Lazarus had been giving me great comfort to see Jesus stop and weep with the bereaved Mary. Joining her in her sorrow. I often revisited this scene in my mind, and its continued reminder that Jesus grieves with us.

As we started reading the beginning of the chapter, my eyes riveted on a section that popped off the page. How had I missed that before?

John 11:5-6 says, "Now Jesus loved Martha and her sister and Lazarus. So, when he heard that Lazarus was ill, he stayed two days longer in the place where he was."

He LOVED them, AND He waited two days! Before Jesus allowed the tragedy of Lazarus's death to occur, the Bible clearly reaffirms that Jesus loved them!

How does this passage read in your life? "Now Jesus loved _____, and He _____?" The second blank of what happened can capture our focus. Or we can shift our gaze back to the phrase leading up to our name. "Now Jesus loved…"

Why does the Bible include Jesus's love for them so clearly, as He stayed where He was, allowing tragedy to hit? For me, He used it to assure my heart that I was still loved, even though He didn't stop the tragedy in my life either.

Is it hard to fathom that dichotomy? Your grief may still be too raw right now. That's normal. When you are able, ask God to show you the truth you need to hear. And like me, you may find it hiding out in a familiar passage just waiting to meet you there.

Prayer

Father,

Thank You that Your Word can answer our heart's uncertainties. Help us bring every question, doubt, or perplexity to You. Draw us to open our hearts to You, that we might experience Your love. Your love that brought Jesus into this world for us. Strengthen our hold on Your unchanging love when our world gets rocked by life.

Abiding in Love
By Elaine Vallario

As we check off the days on our Advent calendar, we continue our ascent to prepare the perfect setting for our holiday memories to be made. Yet as we plan, we know that with each season, year, and even generation that passes, the details of our carefully curated memories will fade.

In this realization, if there is a glimmer of remorse for those forgotten personal touches, remember that God, in His infinite wisdom, did not include meticulous details describing the setting of the first Christmas night. In fact, so little was said about Christ's birthplace that it leaves scholars and historians alike scratching their heads as they try to piece together the humble nativity scene nestled in Bethlehem. But this did not dull its enduring impact on the world.

With intention, God's aim was not to distract us by the things of the world but to engage us with Himself. His plan was simple, and so is His invitation for us to experience it with Him, even in our busy time of planning.

John 15:4, and verse 9 recounts Jesus' invitation to abide in Him. He is inviting us into a relationship with him that endures long past his time on earth. It's a relationship that grows and produces fruit that will nourish the generations to come, even into eternity.

So how does this invitation to abide with Him fit into our celebrations? 1 John 4:12 further explains that if we love one another, His love abides in us and is perfected in us. This glimpse into God's perspective reminds us that, amid the trimmings and treats prepared for the celebration of our King's birth, love is to be placed at the center of the banquet, just as Jesus, lying in a simple manger, is the focal point of every nativity scene.

While it is honoring to God for His people to celebrate His Son's birth with displays of beauty, it is not the dazzling decor that He finds pleasure in, but it is the gentle and humble hearts eager to abide in Him and His love that He delights in. For it is the overflow of love from abiding with Him that rightly adorns the centerpiece of our celebrations.

So, let's spread beauty and prepare to fill not only the bellies and stockings of others, but also their hearts as we share the love of Christ, which comes from the Father. 2 Corinthians 2:12 says, "For the ministry of this service is not only supplying the needs of the saints but is also overflowing in many thanksgivings to God."

To extend your time abiding in the words of our dear Lord, to prepare your heart for the season, read John 15:1-11, 1 John 4:7-15, and 1 Thessalonians 3:11-13.

Prayer

Dear Heavenly Father, in this busy season, may our hearts be fully satisfied by abiding in your presence. Resting in your stillness, we anticipate that the overflow of your love will spread to those around us, not only for the fond remembrances in years to come, but to eternally impact their lives. All honor and glory to God, Amen.

The Gift of all Gifts
By Debbie Prather

One December, a week before Christmas, my high school English class was given an impromptu assignment to write our own obituaries. It was morbid and not fitting for the season. But, it had been a long semester, and maybe our teacher felt like the jingle bell on the elf hat he'd worn that week—hanging by a thread.

Decades later, I see the value of the exercise. I believe he was attempting to teach his squirrelly seniors that we couldn't live fully—with intentionality and to our highest potential—if we weren't acutely aware that the hours on this earth, for everyone, are temporary.

Did we want to be remembered for being gracious and humble or arrogant and angry? Generous and inclusive or tight-fisted and narrow-minded? Careless or considerate? I scratched out clumsy paragraphs to turn the page in quickly, but did give thought, if not fleeting, to how I hoped a summary of my life would someday read. A good teacher, and not just in the classroom, can change everything.

Another December in my twenties, I met a woman named Cheryl, a pastor's wife, at our neighborhood park soon after my husband's job relocated us. I was struggling with loneliness as a stay-at-home mom to littles while being a thousand miles away from the support of family.

Cheryl was kind, insightful, patient, and different—not inclined to the worries of this world—in a way I hadn't known I wanted to be. That month, she invited me to church, where the authenticity of the gospel gripped me for the very first time.

Hearing about God's plan of sending Jesus to be born in Bethlehem, to later die on Calvary, I thought again about how I wanted to be remembered after I was gone, but also how I desired to live—full of goodness, grace, and love.

Goosebumps ran down my arms when the congregation was told that the birth of God's son was established because humankind needed saving and that Jesus is the gift of all gifts, for once and for all eternity: His birth, life, death, and resurrection is the Lord's divine intervention for all people.

I was convicted that my soul required intercession, but pride kept me from immediately expressing that to Cheryl or anyone.

The next day, though, I called my sister, Karen, who continually spread seeds of truth but whose beautiful faith I had previously held at arm's length. I told her I was ready to learn all I could and finally accept Jesus as my Lord and my Savior. She joyfully led me in prayer, and my heart for the past twenty-nine years has never been the same.

A miraculous benefit of saying yes to Jesus is being filled by the Holy Spirit, who gives fulfillment, wisdom, guidance, and peace. New-found humility paved the way for me to share my deepest gratitude both to Karen and to Cheryl for caring enough to lovingly lay out this offering before me and change my eternal destination.

Each year when I put up our tree, play Christmas music, and take in the sights and sounds of the season, I give thanks for the pure radiance of those who selflessly invest in the lives of others. Because of them and because of the ultimate teacher, Jesus, my legacy will always point to His legacy. It's a present I'll share for the rest of my days. It IS the gift of all gifts and a love like no other.

Prayer

Dear Heavenly Father,

Please give us wisdom to number our days and hearts that are in alignment with yours. Thank you that we are called your children because we receive your Son as our Lord and our Savior. May the legacy of our lives be that we never tire or grow weary of generously sharing with others your truth, kindness, love, and grace. It's in your Son's holy name we pray. Amen

The Unwithholdable Love of Christ

By Lisa Ann Gonzalez

The air this time of year is thick—heavy with the weight of expectation. Joy, family, and togetherness hang like ornaments in windows you dare not approach.

For you are the shattered ornament with jagged edges, taken down, forbidden to join. Only watching from the box of tattered yesteryears. You know this ache, this loneliness, this isolation, of watching life through frosted glass; you know what it means to feel the desolation, not belonging there. You learned early.

Perhaps, it was a love turned cruel, or rejection so sharp you still the trace scars in the dark. You began the construction of your walls. Beautiful monuments. In these corridors, you find comfort. You learned that withholding your heart was simply self-preservation. Love extended— was love exploited. So, you locked yourself away—away in a fortress for one.

But what if the One whose birth we celebrate came specifically to shatter that lock? Jesus did not come in triumph. He came in vulnerability. He came down. He came close. He came to the margins where the world had already decided people like you belonged–outside, looking in.

Watch Him move through Scripture like a man possessed by love. He pursues the broken. He eats with the condemned. He touches the untouchable. As if they are the only ones who matter. He found the woman drowning in shame and offered her the truth: You are seen, you are worthy, and you belong. (John 8:10-11)

These were not just gestures. They were invasions. His love ripped through every gate like a force of nature–unstoppable, unrelenting, unafraid. Redemption left behind in place of devastation. Before you were worthy, before you could ask–God gave everything. He gave His Son (Romans 5:8). A love so reckless it cost Him His own HEART.

This is the scandal: not the manger, but the cross. God didn't calculate. He ran. He loves you like a parent who runs into traffic–completely, recklessly, asking nothing in return.

He withheld nothing.

Here is where everything changes for you. You are free. Finally free. Free to love without annihilation. The walls shatter. Not your heart–your fortress. It was never built for a love this fierce. You are held. Completely. Eternally. By a God who loved you when loving you cost everything. You are free to cascade tenderness into a world that starves for it. Your love echoes heaven in you.

This is what Christmas whispers to us. Not just the memory of His coming, but the reality of His presence. Right now. In your guarded place. In your lock -n- heart. He is still pursuing. Still seeking the fortresses. Still breaking through the lies: too much, too little, too damaged, too far gone. He is still saying what He has always said:

Come. You belong here. In my hands, already made whole. My grace is sufficient.

Prayer

Father, forgive me for the ways I have learned to withhold my heart. Teach me to trust in a love I cannot lose—the love of Christ, who came to break open my guarded places and set me free. This Christmas season, help me receive His radical grace and reflect it to a world that desperately needs to know they are loved. Amen.

Let Love Be Love

By Rholyns Mejia

Love is such a vast and powerful virtue. It encompasses about every single relationship there is: God's love for all of us, family, lovers, communities, the people one serves, the love for life, for work, for food, even the love for trivial things. We are all fueled by a certain amount of love that will make it possible to do things no matter how hard they may seem. It is the greatest of all. It is beautiful.

In present times, love's meaning has somehow shifted to mean something else than what the Scriptures say. It has become a thing or a mere word rather than an action or a concept, so beautiful for what it is. Sadly, it is often used in vain. It has become too worldly and materialistic in many ways.

Saying that you love someone does not always show how one expresses what love 1 Corinthians say it is - patient, kind, does not envy, does not boast, is not proud, does not dishonor others, is not self-seeking, is not easily angered, keeps no record of wrongs. Many times, it is a word taken for granted, used to boost charisma, a means to get what someone wants, or just because it is what people say. The beautiful word is losing its meaning when there is not a genuine desire for something.

It is sad to see marriages celebrated in lavish weddings crumble in despair. Or the grand show of a parent's love to a child, only for someone to find them being exploited. Let's not forget a so-called humanitarian donating loads of money out of their so-called love for a charity of their choosing, and later hearing about scandals that are contrary to what their charity stands for. My friends, this is not the "love" that the Scripture describes.

This Advent, I pray that love be shared for what it is. If every person reading this reflects on the true meaning of love and allows it to be the guiding force that would make them want to do something good for themselves, for others, or for anything they believe in, then this world will get to enjoy a more genuine feeling of warmth, comfort, safety, and joy that love brings. Only if we embrace the truest sense of love that we get to share it. With all the negative feelings filling the hearts of many, let the power of love overcome them.

Marriages will flourish with years of beautiful memories. Children will live in an abundance of gratitude and will share the same love with their own children, and their children's children. Charity will come from the smallest of pockets and will make others want to give more. Isn't this the kind of world we would rather have?

First and foremost, let us show ourselves what true love is. Let us not forget the most important person in our lives: ourselves. The only way we can share something is if we have it. Let us fill ourselves with the kind of love that makes us whole as a person. Only then can we express the kinds of action that truly translate to love. Let us start with ourselves, and in the end, we give ourselves the gift of that kind of love that we deserve in return: the one that the Scriptures say it is. Let love be love.

Prayer

Lord, thank you for the love you have for us. I desire to use it as my guiding force to enrich the life you blessed me with. May I continue to spread love so that others who may not have seen it yet will wholeheartedly embrace it. May the power of love be in my heart forever. Amen.

Christmas in Colorado: Hearts Full of Love

By Melissa Lindsey

Snow swirled gently as the old tractor climbed the hill. Snow-covered evergreens sparkled under the morning sun. It was a beautiful, clear morning. The air was crisp, and nine-year-old Sophia could barely contain her excitement—today was the day to pick the family Christmas tree.

Bundled under a heavy quilt beside Auntie Kristen, Sophia rode in the wagon as Uncle Jon drove the tractor through the Colorado mountains. His dog Nikita played alongside in the snow, and Jon pointed out squirrels and deer hiding in thickets. Sophia laughed, full of joy. Several weeks earlier, Uncle Jon told her she was finally old enough to choose the tree, and it had been all she could think about. Now the day had finally arrived!

Jon, Kristen, and Lori (Sophia's Grammy) had moved to Colorado earlier in the year, while Sophia and her mom, Jess, still lived in Massachusetts. This visit was long overdue, and everyone was eager to spend time together. While Grammy and Jess were grocery shopping and planning holiday meals for the week, Jon, Kristen, and Sophia had one special job—bring home the family Christmas tree.

Jon stopped the tractor near a group of evergreens. Sophia leaped from the wagon and ran ahead. "This is it!" she cried, pointing to an almost perfect Blue Spruce. It was full, beautifully shaped, and just the right size for their family room. Jon came over and saw the tag—"Already Sold." He gently pointed it out.

Sophia's face fell. "No! We have to have this one!" she cried. Kristen and Jon exchanged knowing glances. Sophia wasn't easily swayed once her mind was made up. They tried to redirect her to other trees, but her excitement had turned into disappointment. None of the others could compare.

Frustrated, Sophia crossed her arms and stomped. "Why does this always happen? Nothing ever works out right."

Recognizing a teaching moment, Kristen suggested taking a break. It was the season of Advent—a time for preparing hearts and anticipating the arrival of Christmas, the birth of our Savior. She wanted Sophia to understand fully. Jon poured cups of hot cocoa from a thermos they had packed as they sat down at a nearby picnic table. "Sophia," Kristen began, "do you remember the true meaning of Christmas?"

Sophia nodded. "It's when Jesus was born."

"Exactly. The very first Christmas didn't have lights, ornaments, or even a tree. The Bible tells us in Luke 2:7 that when Jesus was born, he was placed in a manger. He didn't even have a bed. Material possessions weren't important at all. The most important thing was love."

Sophia sipped her cocoa thoughtfully. "Then we don't need a tree either, 'cause we have lots and lots of love," she said brightly.

Kristen smiled. "We can still get a tree, but let's not worry if it's perfect. Let's choose to love the one we take home."

Sophia stood. "Let's go. I know which one I want." She marched toward the last row they'd visited and pointed to a small, thin tree that looked like it needed water. "This one just needs love."

Though it wasn't the prettiest, Jon and Kristen agreed—it was perfect because Sophia had chosen it with her heart. As Jon paid, an employee came running. "Hey, remember that big tree you liked? The buyer can't take it and said to give it away. You can have it.

Before Jon or Kristen could answer, Sophia grinned broadly and said, "We don't need it. Please give it to someone who needs love in their heart. We have plenty in our family."

Later that evening, the whole family gathered, and Jon and Kristen shared the story of choosing the tree with Grammy and Jess. Everyone agreed that Sophia had made the perfect choice.

Prayer

God, thank you for the Christmas season and for those who share the love of Christ not only during Advent but every day of the year. Please help us always remember that the condition of our hearts is far more important than decorations or any material possessions.

No Greater Love, No Greater Gift

By Tyann Beenken

I love Christmas—the colors, the sounds, the smells. They all speak a message of faith and family—of love, joy, peace, and hope. The time between Thanksgiving and Christmas has always been one of my favorite times of the year.

Somewhere along the way, however, the peace and joy of the season were overrun by busyness and a sense of overwhelm and stress. I found myself running between office gatherings, Christmas programs, and sports practices, while still trying to meet end-of-year work deadlines, prep the food, bake the cookies, and clean the house before visiting friends and family arrived. No sooner had I gotten the Christmas decorations up than it seemed as though I was taking them down, wondering all the while, "What happened?"

Outwardly, I was being pulled more into the hustle and bustle of the season, where the urgent often trumps the important, and the true meaning of Christmas was getting lost in the shuffle. In my heart, I knew there was more to this season. I found myself longing for a way to slow down, to quiet the noise, calm the chaos, and to center my heart and mind on the Christ of Christmas.

Enter Advent. Until about ten years ago, Advent was not something I was very familiar with. While I grew up in a Christian home and celebrated Christmas, we did not follow a liturgical calendar and celebrate Advent. However, as a busy, stressed-out momma, my heart was drawn to Advent. The practice of purposefully and intentionally setting aside time during the four weeks before Christmas to slow down, to focus on Jesus Christ, and to reflect on the real reason for the season, deeply resonated with my hurried soul.

Over the years, celebrating Advent has become a beautiful tradition in our home. But more than that, it has become a tool to help disciple my children and to point their hearts towards Christ. As they have grown, so has this desire in my heart to help them understand that Christmas is about more than presents, Santa, and a break from school. Yes, it is about the birth of Jesus, but it is about so much more—it is about love.

Because of love, God sent His only Son, Jesus, to restore a relationship that had been broken by sin and to redeem His lost creation. Jesus came to earth, took on our humanity, and yet lived a perfect life. He came to bear our sin and die in our place. Through His life, death, and resurrection, we can be forgiven, stand blameless before God, and receive eternal life. Hallelujah. That is the gift we celebrate at Christmas.

Put up the tree this Christmas season, string the lights, sing the songs, and bake the cookies, but as you do, take the time to quiet your heart, soul, and mind. Ponder the wonder of the season and be humbled by the greatest love ever known. A love so great that God sent His only Son, Jesus, to bear our sin and die in our place so we could bear His righteousness and have everlasting life. There is no greater love, no greater gift, than that.

Prayer

Father God, Amid the busy Advent season, help me not lose sight of the real reason for Christmas. Thank you for loving me so much, for sending Your Son, Jesus, and for the gift of eternal life. This Christmas season, fill my heart with joy, my mind with peace, and my soul with hope because of Your great love. Amen.

Make Room for Love

By Paige Nelson

There is a Facebook group in my city, the Wichita Homeless Initiative, that I am a member of and follow. I don't have a lot of information about who started it or if there is a group that sponsors it or the logistics of it all, but what I do know from the posts I see is that the people who are a part of this group care deeply about our homeless brothers and sisters.

There are requests for donations (food, water, blankets, clothing, gloves, hats, etc.) Some requests are very specific. Some are for more general needs. There are questions about resources for people who find themselves without a place to stay. There are updates about certain people who have been sick or inquiries about homeless friends they haven't seen for a while. Fundraising pages have been set up to help with funeral expenses, along with information about the services. It is a network to help those who have resources connect with those who need them. There are a lot of good people in our community who seek to walk alongside those who find themselves in these situations.

Last December in the last 10 days leading to Christmas, there was a post about a young mother who was living in her car with two young children. There seemed to be a lot to her story, but that night, she needed formula and a place to stay. So many people reached out to help her meet those specific needs, including providing formula and a hotel room for her and her children.

Her plight penetrated my heart, and I couldn't stop thinking about her, the situation she found herself in, and the outpouring of love and grace from this little Facebook community. All of this made me pause to reconsider the Christmas Story.

Our Savior was homeless that Holy Night. Even in the hometown of his ancestors, there was no room for Joseph and Mary. Thankfully, there was a place where animals were usually fed that offered them shelter. We are unsure of whose it was, but, for at least that night, it became home for the Holy Family.

Aside from angel appearances, the heavenly hosts singing, the star, and the magi, Jesus' life had humble beginnings. This, I'm sure, was not an accident, but a part of God's plan to light the way to understanding who the Messiah truly was and is and what He did for us that blessed night and continues to do for us today.

In a modern-day setting, Mary and Joseph could be stranded in their car hoping for a hotel room, a refuge, for at least a night. Instead of shepherds, the people the angel appears before could be those who are living on the streets or in shelters. And where do you think that star would come to rest?

As we move through these last days before Christmas, may we make room for Jesus as we experience and share the Love that came to us at Christmas. Love, in the form of a baby, sent to us because God loves us. Love sent to show us the way to God.

Prayer

Gracious and loving God, thank you for sending your Son so that we can know your Love. Help us, this Advent Season, be more intentional about making room for Love in our busy lives. It's in Your Son's holy and precious name we pray, Amen.

Our Response to God's Gift of Love

By Patti Selvey

May I be honest? Sometimes the Christmas season distracts me from my First Love. Enjoying the worldly delights of twinkling lights on decorated trees, fanciful food, and Christmas carols can sit on the throne of my heart if I'm not careful. Without intention, my gaze lowers from a heavenly-minded perspective, away from the true meaning of Christmas, and onto myself and my own desires. I allow the present urgency to create 'the perfect holiday experience' to blur what's truly important to focus on: God's extravagant gift of love for us.

Remembering God's character and his daily faithfulness resets one's gaze upwards. God is love. He is patient and kind. He is merciful, slow to anger, and quick to forgive. He is all-powerful, all-knowing, and ever-present. He is just, holy, and unchanging. Our God cannot be anything but who he is, true to his Word, fulfilling his promises.

God's love is selfless and sacrificial. Our Heavenly Father sent his Son, Jesus, to earth as a newborn babe with the mission of being the sacrificial lamb to be slain for our sins. That is the gift of all gifts. He is a Redeemer, restoring our relationship with him for all eternity at a great cost to himself.

After receiving the lavish gift of Jesus in our hearts as believers in him, what does the Bible prescribe as a response to God's love?

The Word clearly tells us that we respond by loving others deeply. This deep love overlooks an enormous amount of shortcomings and sins in other believers. Because of this divine love, we can freely forgive others as we have been forgiven. Love does not keep a laundry list of wrongs committed against us.

God's love is humble. This love is demonstrated by deeds carried out in faith, not empty words lacking accompanying action. It allows us to serve others, seeing and meeting a need even when it is not convenient or at a cost to us personally. As God's agents, we bear his image and reflect his radiant love to a hurting world when we serve as Christ served.

As we pause from our Christmas preparations to reflect on God's gift of love, let's ask the Holy Spirit to reveal to us: Who in my circle of influence needs to feel deeply loved today? How can I serve others selflessly in response to God's love? What need can I meet? Who can be encouraged? Who needs to be shown kindness in the name of Jesus? And here's a tough one: Who do I need to forgive? (Please remember, forgiveness does not mean the wrong or offense did not happen. It does not exempt the offender from God's ultimate judgment. It does, however, release the offense out of our control and place it into the just hands of a Righteous God. Forgiveness frees and unburdens our hearts. Another wonderful gift! And as Jesus humbly came, is there someone you need to go to in humility and ask for their forgiveness?

Friend, as we prepare to celebrate Jesus's arrival that fateful night in Bethlehem, may we reflect God's love deeply to others, shining brightly as his disciples into a dark and broken world for the glory of God alone through our attitude and deeds.

Prayer

Heavenly Father, You are worthy of praise! We are grateful for your Son Jesus, your lavish and selfless gift of love to humanity. Help us to love deeply, forgive quickly and completely, and serve others well in your name, Jesus. We want the world to know you and recognize us as your disciples because of our love for one another. Amen.

Loving Kindness
By Vivianna C Welflin

The season of Advent calls me to self-reflect. I have faith that I am living in God's loving kindness, but am I providing loving kindness?

There is no question that I love my husband, my kids, friends, and family. But what does that really mean? I know I'd die for my children, but anyone else? My husband? I think I would. Can I say that about strangers?

I consider the full-time care I provide for my disabled family members in my home, and accept that it is by far the most difficult thing I have ever done, and I struggle to be selfless, but then I think about Jesus' love. I am encouraged.

Even though I ask God to wipe my slate clean each morning, I know I'm going to slip. I'm grateful for God's patience and His grace. I'm wrapped in the endless bounty of God's love, through the sacrifice of His Son, and that's what guides me toward transformation.

John 15:13 refers to the act of laying down one's life for one's friends. Jesus suffered in ways that I cannot comprehend - for my sake. He knows me. That is love, and it's that sacrificial, saving grace that lifts me every day to the difficult task of putting others before myself. I want to love like Jesus loved, even if it's a little at a time.

Prayer

May the love of Father, Son, and Holy Spirit who love us, hear this Advent prayer. Father, continue to guide us to love each other as we celebrate the birth of our King, Jesus Christ. Amen.

Love in Action at Advent

By Elizabeth P. Buttimer

As a child, one of my fondest memories was awakening to the wonderland of Christmas morning. The evergreen tree bedecked with cherished ornaments was draped with colorful paper chains, and our mantle was festooned with fresh garlands and stockings. The aroma of cinnamon, cedar, and Sally Lunn bread baking in the oven filled the air.

I remember staring at the star atop the tree and at the angel ornaments hovering on the branches just below. Seeing them, I could imagine the joyful heavenly choir overlooking the manger as they sang hallelujahs to the newborn King of Kings.

Papa, with his deep and melodic voice, read the scriptures from the Old and New Testaments, heralding our Messiah's birth. When my father prayed, I could feel peace on earth. My heart welled with goodwill to all.

Shortly after those calm moments had passed, it was time to see what St. Nicolas had brought, check the

Christmas stockings, and open presents. That's when the frenzied part of Christmas began.

Ripping into presents, strewing gift wrap on the floor, fighting over a piece of candy, and fussing with my brothers when they teased me, leaving the memory of peace on earth far behind. When the din of squabbling got a little too loud or the likelihood of breaking something during a tug of war became too great, my father would intervene.

He would always solemnly say, "Let us love one another." When he quoted that scripture in a no-nonsense way, we all winced from his reprimand but toned down our fussing, even if a bit begrudgingly.

As an adult, especially around the season of Advent, I have observed that sometimes family occasions bring back those childish fusses or not-so-childish family disagreements or resentments. We're thrown together with kinfolk and in-laws whom we might not see frequently, sometimes for days in close quarters.

Tensions build, tempers flare, patience frays, and peace on earth takes a back seat. We espouse goodwill to all but ask ourselves if we must include disagreeable relatives.

Do we have to include the demanding, the overly critical, or the desperately lonely?

What if someone comes to Christmas dinner, empty-handed, after they promised to bring potato salad? Despite your request for hiking socks, what if a relative regifts to you the reindeer sweater you gave him last year?

Sometimes adults don't squabble as children do, but they can hold grudges, harbor bitterness, or shut out siblings. At Advent, the prelude to Christ's birth, adults may spout outbursts of angry words or hold animosity towards others. "Beloved, let us love one another; for love is from God…" (1 John

I think the shortest distance to another person's heart exists during the Christmas season. The scriptures clearly demonstrate that love is not merely a noun but a verb. More than merely a feeling, love is action—sometimes, powerful, amazing, wonder-working action.

God gave us his only begotten Son. Christ died for us. He gave us the gift of forgiveness, not just on Christmas but every day, forever, "…for God is love." During Advent, I wish for you a glimpse of peace on earth, goodwill to all, and the opportunity to share God's love with others.

Prayer

Almighty God, in this Holy Season, let your love shine through us so that the Star of Bethlehem leads us closer to you and to each other. Help us to love one another as You have loved us. In Jesus name, Amen.

Waiting to Be Loved—and Already Chosen

By Michelle L. Nelson

Matching pajamas, walks in the snow holding hands, mistletoe, evenings by the fire... Do these things evoke feelings of the Christmas season for you? I won't hold it against you if your answer was "yes." It's not hard to get swept away by the "romantic" images of Christmas we see in movies and on social media. In fact, the season can feel quite lonely if we buy into the idea that Christmas isn't Christmas without someone to love.

As a 45-year-old single woman, that message can hit especially hard. But over the years, I've noticed something surprising. Sometimes, when I hear love songs on the radio, they remind me more of God than of a man to love. Not the shallow songs that make love sound effortless, but the ones that speak of sacrifice, devotion, and pursuit. Those lyrics stir my heart to think about the One who has always loved me perfectly–long before I ever knew Him.

Advent is a time of waiting and expectation, and love is at its heart. God's love is not seasonal, conditional, or dependent on circumstances. It's steady, present, and pursuing. The birth of Jesus was love wrapped in human form—God choosing to come near, not because we earned it, but because His nature is love.

When I think about that night in Bethlehem, I'm reminded that divine love doesn't stay distant. It moves toward us. It gives, it shows up, and it sacrifices for the good of others. During Advent, we remember that love came down as an actual promise fulfilled rather than just a fleeting feeling.

So while the world may define love as romance under twinkling lights, I've learned to find it somewhere else. In moments of prayer, when I sense God's presence. In friendships that remind me I'm seen. In opportunities to serve at church. Advent love is not about who's holding your hand but about who's holding your heart.

If this season finds you longing for love, take heart. You already have it. You are deeply loved by a Savior who came for you, thought you were to die for, and is coming again. His love is steadfast and secure, even in seasons of waiting.

As I listen to those same songs now, I can't help but sing along with gratitude—not because I've found earthly love, but because divine love chose me first.

Prayer

Father, thank You for showing us perfect love through Jesus. As we wait and prepare our hearts this Advent season, help us to rest in Your faithful love and reflect it to others. Teach us to find joy not in what we lack, but in knowing we are deeply loved by You. In Jesus' name, Amen.

Wrapped in Love

By Traci Jeffrey

I've tucked away a special Christmas memory, and wear it like a locket close to my heart —small, quiet, but filled with meaning.

I was a stay-at-home mom with three little girls who moved through our home like sunshine—warm and full of life. My husband worked two or three jobs at a time just to keep food on the table and the lights humming. That December, he picked up extra work, hoping to surprise the girls with a Christmas they'd never forget; however, when it came time to be paid, the employer said he didn't have the money to pay my husband, and he would have to wait until next month.

The news hit like a punch to the gut. The girls were old enough to have Christmas dreams, and we were desperate to make them come true.

We worried Christmas morning would feel hollow, and tried not to let our sadness show. We managed to scrape together a very small budget, and I went to work planning how to get the most I could with our meager pennies. I managed to get some presents under the tree, keeping in mind the girl's Christmas wishes.

Still, I felt sad and defeated, and we agonized that Christmas morning would be a disappointment. I heard from other mom friends about the extravagant gifts their children would receive, and I became even more downcast, but continued on. I wrapped every small gift like it were a treasure. I baked cookies with extra cinnamon and played music that made the house feel full. I turned on every string of lights we owned and told myself, "It will be ok." Then came Christmas morning...

The girls tore into their gifts with wide eyes and squeals that bounced off the walls. Paper flew, ribbons unraveled, joy crackled in the air, and when the last package had been opened, my middle child looked up at me with a smile that could light the coldest winter and said, "Mama, this was the best Christmas ever! I got everything I wanted!"

"Me too," shouted the other two girls.

I looked at my husband, and just like that, tears welled up in our eyes—not from sadness, but from the staggering beauty of it all. Love had shown up. Not in the number of gifts, but in the spirit of the day. Not in wrapping paper, but in laughter, togetherness, warmth. We had so little, and yet somehow—miraculously—it felt like more than enough. That morning, love filled the room in a way I could never have imagined, and we learned an important lesson.

Love gives when it costs. Love shows up when there's not enough. Love holds the line when everything else feels fragile. And isn't that exactly what Christmas is about?

God didn't wait for the world to clean up its act. He saw our mess, our empty hands, our not-enough—and gave us everything...His Son, born not into comfort, but into need. Love wrapped not in gold, but in flesh.

I still remember that Christmas as one of the richest I've ever lived. Because love—real love—is never measured by what we have, but by what we give. And that day, we gave all we had, and it was enough. Love always is.

Prayer

Lord, thank You for showing us that true love gives, even in lack. Help us to see the beauty in simple moments and to trust that Your presence is always enough. Teach us to love like You do—freely, fully, and faithfully. Thank You for the gift of Jesus, our greatest joy. Amen.

His Love Is Right On Time

By Olga V. Seredyuk

It was Christmas Eve when I finally placed the little package on Traci's porch. I lingered there for a moment, wondering if I'd waited too long. Inside the box was a pillow printed with a picture of Lulu – her dog, her companion, the one who had died that August. I found the perfect photo, had the pillow made, and wrapped it carefully. It was small and simple, but in my heart, I only wanted to return what had been lost.

Later that night, my phone lit up. Traci's message came through, full of astonishment. Since there'd been no knock or ring of the bell (that felt unnecessary), she texted, "I have no words! By the way, how did you get it on our front porch?"

What I didn't know until then was that Lulu had first arrived on that very same porch thirteen years earlier – on Christmas Eve, too. Traci's oncologist had delivered her there as a gift at the end of chemotherapy. Love, in the form of a small, warm puppy, had once come right to her doorstep. And here she was again – this time on fabric, wrapped in paper, carried by timing I couldn't have predicted would be so sacred. I thought I had been late.

Three months later, I found myself on Traci's porch once more... Less than twenty-four hours earlier, my flight from Munich had been delayed, and I missed the connection in Istanbul. The gate agent had already closed the door ten minutes early. I stood there with tears in my eyes and a carry-on full of cards, drawings, plushies, and bracelets from Ukrainian orphans, each one handmade for Traci, the woman who had prayed for them and was known for saying, "I love you with my whole heart." And that's exactly how she loved. She sat with them, laughed with them, played games, and made one quiet promise: "I'll be back." She kept it for as long as she could, bringing little meaningful gifts — bracelets that read love > fear, olive wood crosses they could hold in their hands, and other tokens of comfort.

Then the seasons changed. The cancer had returned, this time not to be overcome. Traci was placed on home hospice...

Standing there in the restless Istanbul airport, I felt helpless and terrified — caught in a race against time I knew I couldn't win. I wept and pleaded with the help desk agent for a flight as soon as possible. A miraculous reroute through New York appeared and became a long night of waiting, praying, and watching the sunrise through airplane glass.

The sky was pale with morning light as I walked up to the porch again — just as I had on Christmas Eve — and placed the children's gifts there. Suddenly, Traci's family opened the door. "She's awake," they said. I got to say goodbye. Hours later, Traci went silent. Three days after that, she went home to the Lord.

I think about those two porch visits — both full of trembling, offered in faith. In December and again in March, through Traci, God was teaching me to surrender to His love — to see that it is never bound by timing or distance, and that it always finds a way. His love is right on time.

Prayer

Lord, thank You for the grace of holy timing — for arrivals we cannot plan and mercies we don't deserve. When our hearts ache with delay, help us remember that You are still coming near, that You redeem time, and that no love offered in Your name is ever too late. Glory be to the Father, and to the Son, and to the Holy Spirit. Amen.

Love Came Down and Still Shows Up

By Cindy Bennett

The laundry never ends, and maybe that's the point. Here I am again, sorting and folding, doing what love quietly does. Some days I sigh through the piles; other days I offer a prayer between the socks and the t-shirts. But whether weary or content, I find God here in the ordinary, where the sacred often hides in plain sight. A half-finished cup of coffee beside a mountain of laundry reminds me that He meets me in it all.

Love doesn't shout; it serves. It seeks to understand rather than rush to be understood, with steady eye contact that says, "I'm here." It chooses restoration over being right and listens when a child opens up about a real struggle. Sometimes love asks even more. It's stopping at a bench in a hospital courtyard, surrounded by summer flowers, choosing to forgive a family member who broke trust. Love looks like long drives across town, whispered prayers as ambulances pass, or pouring coffee after an argument. Sometimes it means waiting a day before responding to a hard email. Love is trusting Jesus to hold you steady when everything feels like it's falling apart. It grows trust one brave yes at a time. All these glimpses of love echo the truest example we've ever been given. Every small act points back to the greatest One. 1 John 3:16 says, "By this we know love, that he laid down his life for us, and we ought to lay down our lives for the brothers."

That's what Advent reminds me of: Jesus, Love Himself, came near not with a grand display but through humble beginnings. Love came down to dwell among us. Love owns the story, the scars, and the healing. It steps into the mess and shows up in hard places when it would be easier to stay home. As we open our hearts to Jesus, His love settles in and begins to flow through us to others.

This is the invitation of Advent: to pause and make room for Immanuel—God with us—who meets us right in the middle of our everyday lives. He is here in the wrinkled shirts and gentle prayers, the long nights and the steady grace that holds our homes together.

So wherever this season finds you—stirring dinner, wiping tears, or holding on by a thread—remember that the heart of Advent is this: Love came down and still draws near. Jesus is here in every moment, both ordinary and sacred. And when His love shows up, everything changes.

Prayer

Jesus,

You are Love that came down—Immanuel, God with us. Thank You for meeting us in the ordinary and showing us grace in our everyday lives. When life feels heavy, remind us that Your love restores and renews. Help us reflect Your heart so that all we do points back to You. Amen.

The Light of Love

By Francesca Follone-Montgomery, OFS

Love has so many different levels and languages in a variety of relationships, yet they all seem to have some kind of anticipatory excitement for something that is in the plans as a future way to celebrate and honor love. Let's think for a minute about the love that unites two spouses: from dating to engagement to the wedding day, there are moments of expectations, planning, and opportunities to show love along the way. For parents expecting a child, many preparatory steps are taken with anticipation towards the joyful moment of holding the baby in their arms. Soon enough, love is felt through the extended family experience and the overall anticipation of welcoming a baby into the tribe. Finally, the baby arrives, and a new chapter in the family begins. Advent can also be seen as a time of anticipation of being able to receive the joyous presence of a special baby amid our family.

As Christians, we have the beautiful responsibility to use Advent to prepare for the arrival of baby Jesus every year, but let's face it: Christmas is not just a reminder of the birth of the special baby Jesus! It is the celebration of God's love for all humankind! This is why it is a season of light! Love can light up a person's face; it can brighten an otherwise ordinary routine.

Too often, as human beings, we hide our loving nature, and we make bad decisions, forgetting that we have God's love within us. These decisions can lead us to live a life in the darkness instead. The fact is, we should retrieve the light of love and share it by walking and acting as beings of love. We have the wonderful chance to use the Advent season to rekindle their inner light and let it shine for all to see. We need to let it shine to welcome the Light of the world, the Son of our loving God. This is the time for us to show love for God by expressing it towards our own family members and others around us.

Love is one of the words most quoted in the Bible; it is one of the wonderful attributes of God, it is His essence. God gave us part of Himself by sending His only son, Jesus, as the man, the divine son of God, the Holy Spirit. Jesus has experienced life on earth, inclusive of joys and sufferings, friends and familial relationships, fights with the devil, and loving acts, including His sacrificial dying on the cross. There is no greater love than laying down your own life for another. Jesus laid His own life down for all of us! We have access to eternal salvation because of His love.

Reflections on Love

The Christmas season is a reminder of that, too. Too often, we get caught in our daily routine and forget the beauty of being loved by God so much that our own brother and lord, Jesus Christ, has sacrificed his life for us. Advent is a wonderful opportunity for us to prepare with love to welcome Jesus into our hearts and into our home. Every year, we have this reminder, and if we adhere to it, we can live with Jesus in our hearts and in our home every day of our lives.

Jesus is our brother, our most special family member, our God among us! God has created us in His image; we are made with love and of love. So, my message is this: use Advent to rediscover the essence of love and share your inner divine light with others.

For today, do the following:

When you turn on your Christmas decorations, do not forget to also turn on your inner light, smile, and do something with love for others.

Read John 4:8.

Now journal about it: How could you show God to others so that they can see in you His essence of Love?

Reflect on John 15:13 from the previous page: Would you give your life with love for God?

Prayer

Oh, sweet Loving Father, teach us to love you and others as Christ loves us. Help us to prepare for the celebration of Jesus' birth with gratitude for His sacrifice. Let us not dwell on the dark temptations, rather help us to burn them with the light of your essence within us. Guide us to share your love with one another so that we can all experience the warmth of your care. Amen

Looking to *connect* with a community of writers?

www.hopewriters.com

The world needs your *hope-filled* words more now than ever before.

Thinking about *writing* your own book?

www.hopebooks.com

www.ingramcontent.com/pod-product-compliance
Lightning Source LLC
Chambersburg PA
CBHW020246010526
44107CB00002B/122